Data Protection Litigation in the UK

Dedication

To my wife Katherine and
our daughter Eva

To my mother Roisin O'Kane,
and in loving memory of my father John O'Kane

Data Protection Litigation in the UK

Patrick O'Kane

Bloomsbury Professional

LONDON • DUBLIN • EDINBURGH • NEW YORK • NEW DELHI • SYDNEY

BLOOMSBURY PROFESSIONAL

Bloomsbury Publishing Plc
50 Bedford Square, London, WC1B 3DP, UK
1385 Broadway, New York, 10018, USA

Bloomsbury Publishing Ireland Ltd
29 Earlsfort Terrace, Dublin 2, D02 AY28, Ireland

First published in Great Britain 2026

1

British Library Cataloguing-in-Publication Data

A catalogue record for this book is available from the British Library.

ISBN:	PB:	978-1-52653-735-5
	Epdf:	978-1-52653-737-9
	Epub:	978-1-52653-736-2

Typeset by Evolution Design and Digital Ltd (Kent)
Printed and bound by TJ Books, Padstow

MIX
Paper | Supporting responsible forestry
FSC® C013056
FSC www.fsc.org

For product safety related questions contact productsafety@bloomsbury.com

Preface

'Litigation is the pursuit of practical ends within an imperfect system', said Roscoe Pound the famous US lawyer. This is very true in data protection litigation. This book aims to help the reader obtain the best possible result within this imperfect system.

I wrote this book because data protection litigation is a fast growing and developing area of law. For some reason, there has been very little resource to help lawyers in this area. Many of the data protection litigation articles I have read online tend to be dry, legalistic and sometimes pompous.

Data protection litigation can be a maze. The legal framework can be complex and the case law unpredictable. This book tries to guide the reader through the maze.

This book is aimed at people with an interest in data protection litigation. Whilst primarily aimed at lawyers, the book aims to be accessible by anyone. Also, whilst most of the cases I discuss relate to England and Wales, practitioners in Scotland and Northern Ireland should find the content useful.

What is data protection litigation?

Data protection litigation concerns court proceedings brought by individuals or groups claiming loss or damage because of their personal data being mishandled.

This litigation can arise where defendants have:

- caused data to be lost or stolen;
- failed to uphold the rights people have, such as the right to erase their data from systems;
- kept personal data for too long;
- unlawfully shared or sold personal data;
- used personal data behind people's backs without their knowledge; or
- used personal data unlawfully to train artificial intelligence (AI) models.

Data protection litigation is on the rise for several reasons, including:

- **Rights awareness** – People are more aware of their rights than ever before including their rights to sue when companies lose their data.

- **Regulators** – Where regulators go, litigation follows. We have seen regulators across the EU and UK hand down over €5.6 billion in fines since the General Data Protection Regulation (GDPR) dropped in 2018.
- **Technology** – New technology is hungry for personal data. For example, AI often collects the information of ordinary people without their knowledge.
- **Losing it** – When companies accumulate data, they are often prone to losing it. For example, in the UK we have recently seen the Co-op cyber-attack in which all 6.5 million Co-op members had their data stolen.
- **Cybercrime** – Some experts suggest that if cybercrime were a legitimate industry, it would be the third-largest economy in the world just behind the US and China.

Data protection litigation can be messy and unpredictable. It is an area full of contradictions.

- **Tiny cases, vast cases** – Cases can range from tiny nuisance disputes worth £250 (*Driver v CPS*) to large-scale data breach cases with potentially billions of pounds of exposure for defendants.
- **Unpredictable** – The case law still throws up very surprising results.
- **Rights** – People have strong rights to sue if their data are lost or stolen but defendants have numerous potential defences in such claims.
- **The class action casino** – Some of the cases have resulted in tens or even hundreds of thousands of people getting compensation (such as the British Airways data breach litigation from the data breach in 2018 which settled pre-trial). On the other hand, in the Supreme Court case of *Lloyd v Google*, the claimant sought to represent a class of 4 million iPhone users. The claim failed and not one person received compensation.

The book sets out to:

- explain the GDPR and the data protection framework;
- show how data protection cases have been decided in real life;
- show how other competing factors also need to be weighed up in data protection cases (eg, commercial and reputational interests);
- provide essential facts without drowning the reader in information; and
- debunk some of the data protection myths. For example, many have suggested (after the seminal Court of Appeal case of *Farley v Paymaster* in 2025) that the floodgates are now open and that it is easy for claimants to claim compensation in data protection claims. The floodgates are never open in UK law. The UK law is too subtle and discerning an animal for that. It always contains checks and balances. This book sets out to debunk the data protection myths.

Finally, this is an ambitious book in one sense. It seeks to make data protection interesting. People value their rights and they value their privacy. Every day we see new technology emerge which can threaten those rights. For example, this author cannot be the only person who finds the invention of AI glasses creepy and insidious. Data protection litigation is about the intersection between the right to privacy and technology which is increasingly out of control.

I hope you find this book useful.

Patrick O'Kane
London
August 2026

Contents

Table of Statutes

Table of Statutory Instruments

Table of European Legislation

Table of Cases

S

T

U

V

W

CHAPTER 1

Overview of the Data Protection Regime in the UK

INTRODUCTION

1.01 Data protection litigation starts with the data protection legal framework.

In this chapter we look at the data protection framework in the UK. Data protection legislation regulates the processing of personal information.

The two main data protection statutes in the UK are the UK General Data Protection Regulation (UK GDPR) and the Data Protection Act 2018 (DPA 2018). The UK GDPR is the keystone of data protection law. We will consider it in detail. The DPA 2018 supplements the UK GDPR. There are further statutes which we will consider, including the Privacy and Electronic Communications Regulations 2003 (PECR 2003) and the Data (Use and Access) Act 2025 (DUAA 2025).

Data protection litigation in the UK usually arises when an organisation breaches these statutes.

THE UK DATA PROTECTION FRAMEWORK – SUMMARY TABLE

1.02 If you just want to know the basics on the UK data protection framework, read the table below. If you want more detail, then read the full chapter:

Key issues – Your 5-minute guide		
Topic	*Definition*	*Comment*
Data protection litigation in the UK	The GDPR gives you a right to claim compensation from an organisation if you have suffered damage because of a breach of data protection law (GDPR, Article 82)	Under the GDPR, a claimant can sue for: • compensation; and/or • an effective remedy (eg, court order to stop the non-compliant processing (GDPR, Article 79)).
Information Commissioner's Office (ICO)	Regulator enforcing data protection law in the UK	Can fine up to £17.5 million or 4% of global turnover

Topic	*Definition*	*Comment*
EU GDPR	EU Regulation which regulates the processing of personal data	Incorporated into UK law as the UK GDPR
Personal data	Data which relates to an identified or an identifiable human being (GDPR, Article 4)	The word link can be useful in understanding personal data. If data can be linked back to a person, it is likely to be personal data.
Controller	Organisation which determines the purposes and means of the processing of personal data (GDPR, Article 4)	The controller is the organisation which decides how and why the personal data are processed
Processor	Processes personal data on behalf of the controller (GDPR, Article 4)	Does what they are told with the data
GDPR principles	Data must be processed in accordance with principles of: • lawfulness, fairness and transparency; • purpose limitation; • data minimisation; • accuracy; • storage limitation; • security; and • accountability (GDPR, Article 5).	People can sue for breach of any of these principles. They are the key to understanding the GDPR.
Legal basis	Controller must have one valid legal basis in place to process personal data. The legal bases are: • consent; • contractual necessity; • legal obligation; • vital interests; • public task; and • legitimate interests. (GDPR, Article 6)	People can sue if organisations processed their data without having a valid legal basis in place
Special category personal data	Data revealing: • race; • politics; • religion; • genetic/biometric data; • health; • sexuality; and • sex life. (GDPR, Article 9)	Special category data requires more protection. Organisations must identify both a lawful basis (Article 6) and a specific condition (Article 9) to process this data.

Topic	*Definition*	*Comment*
DPA 2018	Works alongside and supplements the UK GDPR	Allows claimant to sue for 'distress' if data rights are infringed
DUAA 2025	Amends and updates the UK GDPR and DPA 2018	Relaxes rules on asserting legitimate interest as legal basis for processing data
PECR 2003	Marketing and cookies rules	People can sue for breach of cookies rules (see **Chapter 13**)

Party One – GDPR – a Refresher

1.03 The General Data Protection Regulation (EU GDPR) was adopted by the EU Parliament and EU Council in 2016 and was effective from 25 May 2018.

It is a mammoth 133-page regulation made up of 99 articles and has been described as 'the most consequential regulatory development in information policy in a generation. The GDPR brings personal data into a complex and protective regulatory regime.' The EU GDPR is a high-profile regulation. The public have a high awareness of the GDPR including their right to sue under the GDPR.

The purpose behind the GDPR is to:

- protect people by giving them rights and control of their personal data; and
- set down rules about how organisations must process that personal data.

To understand UK data protection law, we must first consider the GDPR in detail.

WHICH ORGANISATIONS ARE CAUGHT BY GDPR?

1.04 The GDPR regulates the processing of personal data. The GDPR applies to organisations processing personal data if those organisations are either:

- in the EU; or
- outside the EU but:
  - o offering goods or services to individuals in the EU; or
  - o monitoring the behaviour of those individuals in the EU (eg, by tracking them via cookies).

Post Brexit, the GDPR also applies to companies:

- in the UK; or

- outside the UK but:
  - offering goods or services to individuals in the UK; or
  - monitoring the behaviour of those individuals in the UK (for example, by tracking their online behaviour).

This book is concerned with UK law and the UK GDPR.

GDPR IS AN EU REGULATION – HOW COME IT STILL APPLIES POST-BREXIT?

1.05 The following points explain the position:

- The EU GDPR was effective in all 27 European Union member states from 25 May 2018.
- The UK voted to leave the European Union in the referendum of June 2016.
- The UK left the European Union on 31 January 2020.
- The UK then entered a transition period with the European Union until 31 December 2020.
- At the end of the transition period, the EU GDPR was incorporated into UK law as the 'UK GDPR' under the provisions of the UK European Union (Withdrawal) Act 2018.

The UK GDPR largely incorporates the EU GDPR save for some clarifications and exceptions.

The Information Commissioner's Office (ICO) is the independent supervisory body (or regulator) regarding the UK's data protection legislation.

The ICO says: 'The provisions of the EU GDPR have been incorporated directly into UK law as the UK GDPR. In practice, there is little change to the core data protection principles, rights and obligations. GDPR recitals add depth and help to explain the binding articles. Recitals continue to have the same status as before – they are not legally binding; they are useful for understanding the meaning of the articles.'

When discussing the UK GDPR, this book simply refers to 'GDPR'. The book will specify when it refers to the EU GDPR.

When we consider the GDPR throughout this book, we are doing so from a litigation perspective. We consider how an infringement of the GDPR by an organisation can lead to litigation from an individual seeking to uphold their data protection rights.

WHAT IS PERSONAL DATA?

Personal Data

1.06 We know that data is information, but personal data has an entirely different meaning.

Article 4(1) of the GDPR states:

> 'personal data' means any information relating to an identified or identifiable natural person ('data subject'); an identifiable natural person is one who can be identified, directly or indirectly, in particular by reference to an identifier such as a name, an identification number, location data, an online identifier or to one or more factors specific to the physical, physiological, genetic, mental, economic, cultural or social identity of that natural person.

In other words, personal data is data that is about identifiable human beings.

If something is personal data then individuals have rights and protections over that data and can sue if those rights or protections are violated. If something is not personal data then individuals enjoy no such rights.

Personal Data can be Context-specific and Fact-specific

1.07 It is not always clear when data are personal data. Sometimes it can depend on the context.

For example, let's imagine there is data in a spreadsheet in a doctor's office in Cookstown, a small town in County Tyrone. The data refers to a 102-year-old man who lives in Cookstown who has been suffering with winter flu. The spreadsheet doesn't contain any names. If there is only one 102-year-old man living in Cookstown, then the data in the spreadsheet is that person's personal data because it can be linked back to him.

However, if similar data is on a spreadsheet in a doctor's office in New York, and it refers to a 102-year-old man in New York City, then that data is not personal data (because records show there are approximately 6,000 people over 100 in NYC). Therefore, the reference to the 102-year-old man cannot be linked back to any one individual.

What Kind of Information can be Classified as being Personal Data?

1.08 Personal data can come in a variety of forms. These forms or data are usually referred to as 'categories of data'. Remember, personal data is:

- any information;

- relating to an identified or identifiable natural person ('data subject').

  For example, let's consider a potential data protection claimant called Jatin. He wishes to sue his mobile phone provider Dodgy Phones because the company has suffered a breach and lost all of his personal data.

  Dodgy phones holds a significant amount of personal data including Jatin's:

  - name and address;
  - date of birth;
  - bank account details;
  - credit card details;
  - call recordings from when he phoned to amend his policy;
  - CCTV footage from when Jatin visited one of their outlets;
  - location data collected from Jatin's phone; and
  - data relating to Jatin's health when he submitted an online request for more time to pay his mobile bill due to a recent illness.

All of these items are Jatin's personal data because they:

- are data or information; and
- they relate to Jatin.

The GDPR definition of personal data is very wide. Virtually any data that relates to an individual (including customers, employees and others) is likely to be their personal data.

What does 'Relates to' Mean?

1.09 As we discussed, sometimes the definitions of personal data are not completely clear cut, for example, where a definition states that personal data is:

- any information;
- relating to an identified or identifiable natural person ('data subject').

For example:

- Let's imagine Claire is employed by the civil service.
- Under the GDPR, Claire can ask her employer for access to her personal data.
- Her employer holds information about Claire that is clearly her personal data.
- For example, Claire's personnel file and sickness record are clearly her personal data.

- However, when her employer searches through the data it holds on Claire it finds emails about strategy decisions that Claire was copied into.
- Her employer argues the data is incidental and not 'about' Claire and therefore does not release it to Claire.

In *Deer v University of Oxford* the judge said 'accepting as I do that a person's name is his personal data, it does not follow that every piece of information in a document in which his name appears is his personal information'.

Are Paper Records Regulated by the GDPR?

1.10 Paper records are caught by the GDPR only if they are part of a filing system (eg, they are filed away somewhere in a filing cabinet). In other words, if a company loses looseleaf paper records relating to an employee that were never intended to be filed away then the company could argue the looseleaf records are not subject to the GDPR.

What is a Data Subject?

1.11 A data subject is a human being to whom the personal data relates. Data subjects can claim for breach of their GDPR rights in the courts. For example, a bank is likely to process personal data on a number of different types of data subjects, including:

- customers;
- prospective customers;
- employees;
- job applicants;
- employees from other companies;
- individuals that it tracks on its website using cookies;
- sole traders who perform services for it; and
- visitors to its premises.

What is a Controller?

1.12 Controllers can be sued by data subjects in the courts.

The UK GDPR (Article 4(7)) defines the controller as 'the natural or legal person, public authority, agency or other body which, alone or jointly with others, determines the purposes and means of the processing of personal data.' In other words, it decides how and why the personal data is processed.

The controller bears the ultimate legal responsibility for processing the personal data and it carries most of the risk from litigation.

The controller is the entity that is in the driving seat when it comes to how and why the data is processed.

What are Joint Controllers?

1.13 Joint controllers are two or more organisations that decide how and why personal data are processed together. They are not to be confused with organisations processing data for its own distinct purpose.

Joint controllers have a shared goal or purpose. Together they decide how and why the data are processed.

For example, let's imagine there are two law firms working together on running some online webinars. Together they decide how and why the data are processed. They collect the details of the attendees so they can send them marketing material afterwards. The law firms are joint controllers.

Where there are joint controllers, the data processing is conducted for a common purpose (ie, a shared goal or a joint enterprise).

Under Article 82(4) of the GDPR, it says 'Where more than one controller …, are involved in the same processing and where they are … responsible for any damage caused by processing, each … shall be held liable for the entire damage in order to ensure effective compensation of the data subject.'

What is a Processor?

1.14 Usually, a processor is a company performing a service on behalf of a controller organisation for money under a contract, and part of that service includes processing data for the controller.

Processors can be sued by data subjects in the courts.

The UK GDPR defines a processor at Article 4(8) as: a natural or legal person, public authority, agency, or other body which processes personal data on behalf of the controller.

Companies invariably use third parties to help them carry out their business operations. These companies are sometimes referred to as vendors or suppliers. If these vendors or suppliers process personal data on behalf of the controller company then they are processors under the GDPR. There are an almost infinite number of services that may be provided by processors from cloud services to providers of AI technology, to IT security providers, to payroll providers.

What does 'Processing' Personal Data Mean?

1.15 Processing is defined at Article 4(2) of the GDPR and means 'any operation or set of operations which is performed on personal data'. In other words, 'Processing means taking any action with someone's personal data.'

The definition of processing is very wide. Anything that a company does with personal data counts as processing it, including 'collection, recording, organisation, structuring, storage, adaptation or alteration, retrieval, consultation, use, disclosure by transmission, dissemination or otherwise making available, alignment or combination, restriction, erasure or destruction'.

What are the Special Categories of Personal Data?

1.16 Special category data is a more sensitive type of personal data. If an organisation loses special category data, then it will usually be easier for a claimant to obtain compensation against the organisation.

For example, imagine a solicitors firm called 'Loose Law' is hacked.

- A client file relating to their client David goes out into the wild.
- David is a new client and therefore the file only contains David's email address and phone number but no further data.
- During the hack Loose Law also lose Angelica's file.
- Angelica's file contains details about her unfair dismissal claim against her employers including details about her mental health and ethnicity.
- David and Anglica sue Loose Law.
- Given that Angelica's special category data have been lost, she has a stronger claim in damages than David against Loose Law.

There are certain categories of personal data that require extra protection under the GDPR, Article 9. These categories of personal data are known as the special categories of personal data and relate to:

- race;
- politics;
- religion;
- philosophical beliefs;
- trade union membership;
- genetics;
- biometrics;

- sex life; and
- sexual orientation.

The Right to sue under the GDPR

1.17 The GDPR gives data subjects rights to make a claim in court for compensation for infringement of the regulation.

Article 82(1) says 'Any person who has suffered material or non-material damage as a result of an infringement of this Regulation shall have the right to receive compensation from the controller or processor for the damage suffered.'

The GDPR does not set the level of compensation that a data subject could receive for infringement as this is set by the courts.

Recital 146 of the GDPR says that 'Data subjects should receive full and effective compensation for the damage they have suffered.' Recital 146 is not often cited in court in the author's experience. However, it is useful for judges to know about Recital 146 when they are being addressed on quantum and the fact that compensation under the GDPR must be not only 'full' but 'effective'.

It is difficult to see how some of the micro awards that have been handed down in UK courts are consistent with Article 82 and Recital 146. For example, in *Geoffrey Driver v Crown Prosecution Service*, the High Court awarded a claimant only £250 in damages when he experienced distress following a security breach which compromised his data.

We will look in more detail in **Chapter 2** about the meaning of material and non-material damage.

Compensation can be Claimed against Processors

1.18 Claimants can sue either the controller, the processor, or both, for breach of the GDPR. Processors can only be sued under certain parts of the GDPR. They are usually only liable if they have caused a data breach (ie, they have caused data to be lost or compromised). Controllers can be sued more widely for breach of more of the provisions.

Article 82(2) says 'Any controller involved in processing shall be liable for the damage caused by processing which infringes this Regulation. A processor shall be liable for the damage caused by processing only where it has not complied with obligations of this Regulation specifically directed to processors or where it has acted outside or contrary to lawful instructions of the controller.'

Processors can be liable for security breaches. Under Article 32(1) of the GDPR, the processor must put security measures in place to keep the personal data safe. It says 'the processor shall implement appropriate technical and organisational measures to ensure a level of security appropriate to the risk'.

For example, Fiona's data are lost in a data breach when her employer, Big Corp, is the victim of a ransomware attack. Big Corp's is the controller and its data are hosted by a processor called Tech Platform. Tech Platform is responsible for the breach due to having inadequate security in place around the data. Fiona decides to sue both Big Corp and Tech Platform for causing her data to be lost in the hack.

Multiple Defendants in a Claim

1.19 What happens when there is a complicated breach of the GDPR involving multiple parties and there is finger pointing between the defendants in relation to liability?

GDPR Article 82(4) sets out that each controller or processor can be liable for the entire damage. In other words, the defendants are jointly and severally liable.

If the claimant has established that the GDPR has been breached and that it has suffered damage, then the claimant does not need to spend time in the case showing which defendant is responsible for each aspect of the damage. Once the claimant has established the breach and loss was caused the defendants, it is in a strong position and can obtain compensation. The claimant can let the defendants fight amongst themselves about who is to blame for each aspect of the data processing. In other words, the claimant is just 'throwing the ball' in and letting the defendants fight amongst themselves about who is at fault for each aspect of the data processing.

Anonymisation

1.20 The terms anonymised data and anonymisation are bandied around very liberally. However, for data to be truly anonymous and therefore outside the scope of the GDPR, there is quite a high bar for anonymisation. The ICO says 'Anonymisation is about reducing the likelihood of a person being identified or identifiable to a sufficiently remote level.' It requires that the data be permanently 'rendered anonymous'.

The author suggests that the data must be rendered anonymous such that the controller could not de-anonymise the data even if it wanted to. Rather like Humpty Dumpty in the children's nursery rhyme, the data must be anonymised to such a degree that 'all the King's horses and All the King's men couldn't put it back together again'. If the data are anonymised then no one could put the pieces back together again.

What does Anonymisation Mean in the Context of Data Protection Claims?

1.21 You may see defendants claim that there has been no loss or damage because the personal data in question has been anonymised. Claimants should check that the defendant is applying the proper standard of anonymisation under the GDPR and by the ICO.

Pseudonymisation

1.22 Pseudonymisation 'refers to techniques that replace, remove or transform information that identifies people, and keep that information separate'. For example, if Patrick and Sean's names are on a payroll database that is about to be sent to a third-party supplier. The controller removes Patrick and Sean's names and replaces them with the codes 007 and 008, respectively. The data have been pseudonymised and there is less of a risk when they are sent to the supplier. The data are still subject to the GDPR.

What is a Personal Data Breach under the GDPR?

1.23 Breaches of security are perhaps the most common basis upon which data protection claims are founded. These are claims where the claimant alleges that the defendant has caused their data to be lost or compromised.

GDPR, Article 4(12) says '"personal data breach" means a breach of security leading to the accidental or unlawful destruction, loss, alteration, unauthorised disclosure of, or access to, personal data transmitted, stored or otherwise processed'.

Privacy Notices

1.24 Claimants can potentially sue a defendant if they are not advised properly in privacy notices how their data are processed.

If an organisation has not told an individual about the data processing it is doing, then it can be sued for breaching the claimant's right to be informed. Organisations have obligations to tell individuals about the data they are processing in their privacy notices. If they breach these obligations then the individuals can potentially sue for breach of the GDPR.

The rules on the types of information that must be provided to data subjects about how their data are processed fall into two categories:

(1) **The organisation collected the data directly from the data subject**. For example, if a company collects data from a data subject, it must tell the

data subject about who it is and how long it intends to keep the data. When personal data is collected directly from the data subject, then the privacy notice information must be provided at the time the data is collected.[1]

(2) **The organisation collected the data from other sources**. For example, if a company did not collect data from the data subject but obtained it from other sources, then it must always tell the data subject about why it is using the data. It must also explain the lawful basis it is relying on for the processing. When collecting data from other sources, the privacy notice information must be provided 'within one month' at the latest.[2]

Please consult Articles 13 and 14 of the GDPR for more details.

There are some exemptions to providing privacy notice information, including where the data subject already has the information. These exemptions are set out at Articles 13(4) and 14(5) of the GDPR.

Transferring Personal Data outside the UK

1.25 If the rules on data transfers are breached, then a data subject can sue for compensation under the GDPR if they can show loss or damage because of that breach.

A company is caught by the GDPR. What must it do in order to be allowed to send personal data from the UK to another country?

In order for the transfer to be allowed, it must fall into one of the following three categories[3]:

(1) **safe country** – data is going to a safe country (ie, a country that the UK Government considers safe); or

(2) **appropriate safeguard** – there is an appropriate safeguard in place (eg, although the data is being sent to a country that is *not* on the UK's list of safe countries, there is a contract between the sending and receiving companies covering data protection); or

(3) **exception** – there is an exception in place (eg, the company has the consent of the data subject to send the personal data outside the UK).

We do see some litigation where claimants sue because the defendants sent the claimant's data to a third country in a manner that was not complaint with the GDPR rules.

1 GDPR, Article 13(1).
2 GDPR, Article 14(3)(a).
3 GDPR, Articles 45–49.

The Data Protection Principles

1.26 People can sue if data controllers do not handle their data in line with the data protection principles.

The principles relating to the processing of personal data are the most important part of the GDPR. **Chapter 14** of this book examines the principles in more detail.

In deciding whether the GDPR has been infringed and whether a claim will succeed, you can use the principles to guide you on whether the activity is consistent with these principles. If a defendant has breached one or more of these principles, then they may be subject to litigation.

The principles are set out at Article 5 of the GDPR.

1. Lawfulness, fairness and transparency

1.27

> Personal data shall be processed lawfully, fairly and in a transparent manner in relation to the data subject.

For example, a mother claimed successfully against a school in the case of *ST (a minor) v L Primary School*,[4] when a letter was issued about her daughter's special educational needs without the mother's consent. The data was not therefore processed lawfully. The daughter was awarded £1,500 and the mother was awarded £3,000.

2. Purpose limitation

1.28

> Personal data shall be collected for specified, explicit and legitimate purposes and not further processed in a manner that is incompatible with those purposes.

In the European Court of Justice (ECJ) case *Österreichische Post AG*,[5] the controller collected information about individuals and then enriched that data by estimating what their political affinity was before offering the data to the political party's advertisers. This violated the rule on purpose limitation. While ECJ cases are no longer binding on UK courts, they are often persuasive.

3. Data minimisation

1.29

> Personal data shall be adequate, relevant and limited to what is necessary in relation to the purposes for which it is processed.

4 *ST (a minor) v L Primary School* [2020] EWHC 1046 (QB).
5 Case C-300/21, *UI v Österreichische Post*, ECLI:EU:C:2023:370.

Firms cannot use more data than is necessary for a particular purpose.

4. Accuracy

1.30

> Personal data shall be accurate and, where necessary, kept up to date.

6. Security

1.31

> Personal data shall be processed in a manner that ensures appropriate security of the personal data, including protection against unauthorised or unlawful processing and against accidental loss, destruction or damage, using appropriate technical or organisational measures.

Security has always been fertile ground for data protection litigation. **Chapter 7** of this book examines the security principle in more detail.

7. Accountability

1.32

> The Controller shall be responsible for, and be able to demonstrate compliance with the above principles.

Firms should keep records of the way in which they process personal data in compliance with the GDPR, in case a regulator ever asks for evidence of their data processing.

Fines

1.33 The maximum fine for breach of the UK GDPR is 4% of global annual turnover or £17.5 million (whichever is highest for a particular company).

Organisations should always keep the principles in mind when building a data protection programme within their company.

The Legal Bases for Processing Personal Data

1.34 Think of the legal bases like rock climbing. One would never engage in rock climbing without having proper support in place. Similarly, an organisation can never process personal data without having a legal basis in place.

When a company processes personal data relating to a particular individual, it must have a legal basis in place that allows it to carry out each aspect of the personal data processing.

No company can ever process personal data unless it has a legal basis in place. Doing so can leave it open to being sued by individuals.

A legal basis

1.35 The legal bases for processing appear at Article 6 of the GDPR, as set out below:

- Consent of the data subject – The data subject has given consent to the processing of his or her personal data for one or more specific purposes. Under Article 4(11) of the GDPR, consent is:

  > Any freely given, specific, informed and unambiguous indication of the data subject's wishes by which he or she, by a statement or by a clear affirmative action, signifies agreement to the processing of personal data relating to him or her.

- Contractual necessity – Processing is necessary for the performance of a contract to which the data subject is party or in order to take steps, at the request of the data subject, prior to entering into a contract.
- Legal obligation – Processing is necessary for compliance with a legal obligation to which the Controller is subject.
- Vital interests of an individual – Processing is necessary in order to protect the vital interests of the data subject or of another natural person.
- Performance of a task in the public interest
- Legitimate interest of a firm – Processing is necessary for the purposes of the legitimate interests pursued by the controller or by a third party, except where such interests are overridden by the interests or fundamental rights and freedoms of the data subject.

There is no one legal basis that works better than the other available legal bases but it is up to an organisation to judge which legal basis is most appropriate in the circumstances based on the type of data processing it is doing and on its relationship with the data subject.

Cookies

1.36 Cookies are small pieces of information that are stored on your device by a website. These allow the website to track your movements on the website. This is supposedly to make things more convenient for you. For example, it may prevent you from having to log in to the site every time you are on it.

The rules on cookies are set out in the UK PECR Regulations. The GDPR is also in play if the cookies process personal data.

The ICO states:

The basic rule is that you must:

- tell people the cookies are there;
- explain what the cookies are doing and why; and
- get the person's consent to store a cookie on their device.[6]

Cookies must not be installed until the company has obtained the appropriate consent from the website user. It must provide enough information on the site near the cookie consent to explain how the cookie data is processed.

The consent required is the GDPR standard of consent (ie, it must be freely given, specific, informed and one must opt in).[7]

We consider cookies litigation at **Chapter 13**.

There have been some claims taken for breach of the rules on cookies and consents including the case of *RTM v Bonne Terre Ltd & Anor*[8] where the claimant, a recovering gambling addict brought a claim against an online gaming company alleging that the consent it obtained for its use of cookies was an invalid consent. The case went to the Court of Appeal. We consider this in detail at **Chapter 13**.

Data Subject Rights

1.37 People can sue if companies do not abide by the rules on data protection rights which are set out at Articles 12-23 of the GDPR.

Individuals have certain rights over personal information that organisations hold on them including:

- The right of access.
- The right to rectification.
- The right to erasure.
- The right to restrict processing.
- The right to data portability.
- The right to object.
- Rights in relation to automated decision making and profiling.

Rights can be difficult and expensive for companies to deal with. We are going to look at each right in turn. We will look at some practical steps for dealing with GDPR rights at the conclusion of the chapter.

6 Ico.org.uk – Cookies and similar technologies
7 GDPR, Articles 4(11), 7.
8 *RTM v Bonne Terre Ltd & Anor* [2026] EWCA 488.

Rights requests – the formalities

1.38

(a) **Must be answered within one month**. GDPR rights requests must be responded to 'within one month'.[9]

(b) **Customers can make a request by email, letter or on the phone.**[10] They can be made in any format including orally, by email or even to a company via Twitter. Individuals do not have to complete a company access request or erasure form for a request to be valid. They can make a request in any format they choose.

(c) **Companies usually must deal with these requests**. A company can only refuse to act on a request if it is:

- manifestly unfounded; or
- manifestly excessive.[11]

(d) **Check the person's identity**. Companies should use 'all reasonable measures' to verify the identity of people making GDPR rights requests.[12] In other words, it should take reasonable steps to verify the person's identity before complying with their request.

(e) We go into these rights in more detail in **Chapter 8**.

THE DATA PROTECTION ACT 2018

1.39 The Data Protection Act 2018 (DPA 2018) is an important part of the UK's data protection framework. The DPA 2018 refines and supplements the UK GDPR.

Section 169 sets out that people who have are seeking compensation for breach of their data protection rights under the GDPR can claim for distress.

THE DATA USE AND ACCESS ACT 2025 (DUAA 2025)

1.40 The ICO states that the DUAA 2025 'amends, but does not replace, the UK General Data Protection Regulation (UK GDPR), the Data Protection Act 2018 (DPA) and the Privacy and Electronic Communications Regulations (PECR).'

The DUAA 2025 was designed to reduce some of the red tape around the GDPR but also to protect the information rights of individuals.

9 GDPR, Article 12(3).
10 GDPR, Article 12(3).
11 GDPR, Article 12(5).
12 GDPR, Recital 64.

For example, it allows companies to:

- use cookies to collect information without seeking consent in some cases such as when it is using them to improve its website;
- more easily rely on the legal basis of legitimate interests when conducting automated processing by a computer or a system (which is particularly useful in the context of AI); and
- reuse the information for scientific purposes without putting it in a privacy notice if doing so would involve a disproportionate effort.

The DUAA 2025 also makes it clear that when someone makes a subject access request under the GDPR, the controller must only make a 'make reasonable and proportionate searches' for their data.

Sometimes data protection claims are brought by claimants alleging that the defendant breached the rules on data subject access requests. Often these cases allege that the defendant did not search for or provide all of the data the claimant demanded under Article 15 of the GDPR. The DUAA 2025 will make it easier for defendants to defend those claims as they can now assert that they conducted a reasonable and proportionate search.'

TAKEAWAYS

1.41

- The UK GDPR and the Data Protection Act 2018 are the key statutes in UK data protection law.
- Controllers and processors can be sued for breach of these statutes.
- Claimants can sue for non-material damage such as distress when their data protection rights have been infringed.
- Claimants can sue if their personal data are compromised. If special category data (eg, data relating to race, health, sexuality, political opinions) have been compromised, then the claimant is likely to have an even stronger claim against the defendants.
- The right to sue under the GDPR is set out at Article 82.

CHAPTER 2

What Types of Damage are Recoverable under the GDPR?

INTRODUCTION

2.01 In the first part of this chapter, we will look at what the GDPR says about the types of compensable damage under the GDPR and the Data Protection Act 2018. In the second part, we examine the case of *Farley v Paymaster*, the leading authority on compensable damage in the UK.

PART I
DAMAGES CLAIM

2.02 The main law is set out in Article 82 of the GDPR. The purpose of Article 82 is to give people full compensation when their GDPR rights have been infringed without having to disentangle which controller or processor is responsible for what.

Damages Claims Summary Table

2.03 This table gives a brief overview of the key concepts before we explore the concepts in more detail.

Claims for damages under GDPR		
Topic	*In a nutshell*	*In practice*
• What does the GDPR say?	• Article 82(1) of the GDPR says 'Any person who has suffered material or non-material damage' can get compensation	• Recital 146 of the GDPR says compensation should be 'full and effective'
• What are the rules for claiming for distress?	• Article 168 of the DPA 2018 says that claimants can claim for distress	• DPA 2018 supplements the GDPR • Broad definition of 'damage'

Topic	*In a nutshell*	*In practice*
• Can individuals sue only data controllers?	• Under the GDPR, Article 82(1) individuals can sue controllers and processors	• If there is a data breach, it might make sense for them to sue the processor if the controller has no money
• What if there is data protection litigation taken against multiple organisations?	• By virtue of the GDPR, Article 82(4), there is joint and several liability • In other words, if more than one company is responsible for causing a data protection breach, the claimant can claim against any one of them	• If one organisation can't pay, the others must cover the full amount
• What is the limitation period under the GDPR?	• 6 years • 3 years if claiming personal injury	• Personal injury can arise in a data claim such as psychiatric damage due to unlawful processing (eg, psychiatric damage in a data claim could arise if false allegations were printed in a newspaper)
• What does the UK case law say about which kinds of damages are recoverable?	• *Farley v Paymaster (1836) Ltd* [2025] EWCA Civ 1117 – Court of Appeal says a claimant does not even have to suffer distress to obtain compensation	• Claimant can get compensation for fear of the consequences of a data breach if the fear is well-founded
• Which procedures do defendants rely on?	• Defendants often seek to: ○ strike out on the grounds that there is no reasonable prospect or success; or ○ assert the claim is an abuse of process.	• No reasonable prospect of success may be harder now post *Farley v Paymaster* (see below)

Compensation can only be obtained under the GDPR through the courts. The Information Commissioner's Office (ICO) has no power to issue compensation for breaches of the GDPR.[1]

1 See ICO, 'Taking your case to court and claiming compensation', https://ico.org.uk/for-the-public/data-protection-and-journalism/taking-your-case-to-court-and-claiming-compensation/.

Have the Courts awarded Low Awards of Damages in Data Protection Claims?

2.04 Awards from courts have not been high in recent years and therefore parties often feel a commercial imperative to settle these claims.

For example, a defendant may not want to fight a case relating to a data breach claim when they are in a weak position on liability and when the claimant is only claiming £500. The defendants may find it may be less expensive to settle the claim early for a low sum without incurring legal costs. Also, fighting cases can sometimes lead to more publicity and can encourage more claimants to come out of the woodwork.

As Lord Justice Warby said in the *Farley v Paymaster* case, 'litigation of limited merit can be used as a weapon of oppression.'[2]

Are Data Protection Claims Becoming More Common?

2.05 More data protection claims are being taken than ever before for several reasons including:

- **The GDPR requires organisations to inform people how their data are processed**. The GDPR requires controllers to be much more transparent in their privacy notices.
- **The GDPR requires organisations to 'fess up' when data are lost**. Controllers must also report data breaches (under Article 34) of the GDPR where they cause a high risk to the data protection rights and freedoms of the data subject.
- **The GDPR is well known to the public**. The GDPR has a higher name recognition than many other regulation and people are much more aware of their rights to sue for GDPR breaches.

What is the Logic Behind the Rules on Claiming Compensation under Article 82 of the GDPR?

2.06 The EU wants to ensure that individuals enjoy extensive rights over their personal data. Pre-GDPR, companies could play fast and loose with data without fear of serious consequences. The Wild West era with data is over. The GDPR makes it easier for claimants to obtain compensation for breach of their data protection rights.

2 *Farley v Paymaster* (1836) Ltd [2025] EWCA Civ 1117, para 104.

MYTH BUSTING – EXPLODING SOME MYTHS ABOUT DAMAGES UNDER THE GDPR

Myth busting

2.07

- **Claimants can only claim for a recognised psychological injury** – Wrong. Claimants can claim for distress under the GDPR/Data Protection Act 2018 (DPA 2018). In fact, claimants do not need even to suffer distress to be eligible for compensation. After the Court of Appeal case of *Farley v Paymaster* (which is considered below in detail), claimants can be eligible for compensation for fear of the consequences of breach if it is well-founded.
- **Claimants cannot claim for material damages under GDPR/DPA 2018** – Incorrect. The GDPR allows claimants to claim for material damage such as economic loss. Whilst this does not arise too often in data protection, there are some claims which include an economic loss element.

WHAT KINDS OF DAMAGES CAN BE CLAIMED?

2.08 These rules are set out in the GDPR and are supplemented by the DPA 2018.

Article 82(1) of the GDPR says that 'Any person who has suffered material or non-material damage as a result of an infringement of this Regulation shall have the right to receive compensation from the controller or processor for the damage suffered.'

Material Damage

2.09 The DPA 2018 sets out in section 169(5) that damage includes financial loss.

Material damage is usually financial loss, but it can include other things such as:

- economic disadvantage;[3]
- physical injury; and
- psychological Injury.[4]

For example, let's say Pete is a plumber in Dulwich. A website posts false comments alleging that Pete is incompetent. The comments breach the GDPR

3 GDPR, Recital 85.
4 *Farley v Paymaster*, para 52.

accuracy principle. The plumber could potentially recover damages for economic loss if the breach caused him to lose customers.

Non-material Damage and the Ability to Sue for Distress

2.10 Non-material damage covers things like:

- distress;
- anxiety;
- stress; and
- irritation,

which stop short of physical or psychological injury.

Recital 85 sets out other non-material damage that is compensable under the GDPR, for example:

- limitation of rights;
- discrimination;
- identity theft or fraud;
- unauthorised reversal of pseudonymisation;
- damage to reputation;
- loss of confidentiality of personal data protected by professional secrecy; or
- any other social disadvantage.

For example, Amanda's personal data are held by her local doctor. Her doctor's IT systems are hacked. Amanda's data end up on the dark web. Amanda is very anxious about this and it has affected her mood and sleep. Amanda sues her doctor for the stress and anxiety she has suffered.

How does GDPR want us to Approach the Subject of Damage?

2.11 The GDPR wants us to interpret damage broadly.

We can look at the GDPR, Recital 146 (the recitals give further colour and explanation to the GDPR provisions).

Recital 146 says:

- 'Data subjects should receive full and effective compensation for the damage they have suffered'; and

- 'The concept of damage should be broadly interpreted in the light of the case-law of the Court of Justice in a manner which fully reflects the objectives of this Regulation.'

The compensation must not only be *full* – in terms of the amount of damages – but *effective* – in terms of adequately compensating the data subject.

This author argues that some of the micro awards we have seen in data protection cases are not full and effective awards. For example, in *Driver v CPS*[5] a local politician suffered a data breach in respect of his data, but the court only awarded £250. The author suggests that the award is not 'full and effective' compensation.

Can Distress be Claimed?

2.12 The DPA 2018 says at Article 168(1) that 'non-material damage' includes distress and therefore people can claim under the GDPR and the DPA 2018 for distress.

What is distress?

2.13 Distress is defined in the Oxford English Dictionary as 'severe mental emotional pain or worry'.

There is a spectrum of distress from upset to a very severe and debilitating worry (which falls short of material damage such psychiatric injury which is considered below).

The Court of Appeal in *Farley v Paymaster* said that distress is 'typically, and most commonly, used as an umbrella term for various forms of emotional harm (including, for instance, stress and anxiety)'.[6]

CAN A DATA SUBJECT SUE A DATA PROCESSOR AS OPPOSED TO A DATA CONTROLLER FOR BREACH OF DATA PROTECTION LAW?

Can a data subject sue a data processor instead of a controller?

2.14 Yes. A claimant can sue a processor instead of (or as well as) a controller as part of a data protection claim.

Article 82(1) says:

> Any person who has suffered material or non-material damage as a result of an infringement of this Regulation shall have the right to receive compensation from the controller **or processor** for the damage suffered.

5 *Driver v CPS* [2022] EWHC 2500.
6 *Ibid*, para 52.

WHEN CAN CLAIMANTS SUE A PROCESSOR?

2.15 Article 82(2) of the GDPR says:

> A processor shall be liable for the damage caused by processing only where it has not complied with obligations of this Regulation specifically directed to processors or where it has acted outside or contrary to lawful instructions of the controller.

As the ICO has said:

> A processor will only be liable for the damage if:
>
> A. It has failed to comply with UK GDPR provisions specifically relating to processors. For example, if the processor caused a data breach of the claimant's data.
>
> B. It has acted without the controller's lawful instructions, or against those instructions. For example, if the processor acted outside the controller's instructions and used the data for its own purposes.

In many cases, however, the claimant might not know who the processor is nor ever heard of them. The claimant is much more likely to know and have a relationship with the controller. When a claimant sues under GDPR the controller is more likely to be in the litigation firing line.

MULTIPLE DEFENDANT CASES?

2.16 The GDPR says that where multiple defendants are jointly liable for a breach of the GDPR, the claimant does not have to prove which defendant was responsible for each aspect of the breach. The claimant can sue any one of them for all the damages. Once the case is over, the defendants can fight amongst themselves over who is liable for what.

In other words, every defendant involved is responsible for all the compensation, not just their slice. If one can't pay, the others must cover the full amount (see the GDPR, Article 82(4)).[7]

OFF THE HOOK? A POTENTIAL DEFENCE

2.17 If there are multiple processors and controllers, they are not liable for damages if they can prove they were not responsible in any way for the damage.

7 GDPR, Article 83(4) says 'Where more than one controller or processor, or both a controller and a processor, are involved in the same processing and where they are … responsible for any damage caused by processing, each controller or processor shall be held liable for the entire damage in order to ensure effective compensation of the data subject.'

Article 82(3) says 'A controller or processor shall be exempt from liability … if it proves that it is not in any way responsible for the event giving rise to the damage.'

Further Defendant Strategies for Dealing with Data Protection Claims

2.18 Under the Civil Procedure Rules (CPR) 3.4, the court may strike out a case on several grounds, including if the claim:

- discloses no reasonable grounds for bringing or defending the claim;
- is an abuse of the court's process; and
- the claimant has failed to show that it is more likely than not the claim would succeed at trial.

Defendants often make applications to strike out data protection claims before they come to a full hearing on some of the grounds under CPR 3.4.

WHAT ABOUT CAUSATION?

2.19 Article 82(1) says that 'Any person who has suffered material or non-material damage as a result of an infringement of this Regulation shall have the right to receive compensation from the controller or processor for the damage suffered.'

A claimant must prove three elements before their GDPR claim can succeed:

- a breach of GDPR;
- loss or damage; and
- causation (ie, that the GDPR breach caused the damage).

Example:

- David sues his mobile provider 'Big Mobile' after they were hacked and lost David's personal data.
- David sues for general damage for the anxiety he suffered as a result of the breach.
- David also sues for material damage (ie, economic loss).
- David says that the data breach caused two fraudulent transactions on his credit card which left him out of pocket for £350.
- David can prove that Big Mobile caused the data breach.
- At court, Big Mobile claims that the fraudulent transactions would have happened anyway and that it has 'nothing to do with the data breach'.
- The court award David £1,500 for the material damage claim.

- David's claim for material damage fails.
- Whilst he can show that Big Mobile caused the data breach, he is unable to show that the fraudulent transactions were caused by the data breach.

LIMITATION PERIOD UNDER THE GDPR

2.20

- six years for a GDPR claim; and
- three years for personal injury, for example, a GDPR breach causing some psychiatric injury.

PART 2
THE KEY CASE ON DAMAGES

2.21 The case of *Farley v Paymaster Ltd* is a key case on data in UK data protection law. It has lowered the bar for claimants in terms of the damage and loss they must prove to obtain compensation.

FARLEY OVERVIEW

2.22 They key points in the *Farley v Paymaster* case are summarised in the table below.

The key case of *Farley v Paymaster* – overview and summary		
Topic	*Answer*	*Paragraph(s) within the Farley judgment*
What are the three main takeaways in the *Farley* case	1. Sending data to the wrong person can lead to compensation even if no third party sees it 2. A person can claim for anxiety or even annoyance as long as they can objectively show these 3. Minor damage can still be compensable	93, 76
Is there a threshold of seriousness to claim compensation for breach of the GDPR?	There is no threshold of seriousness for a person to get compensation under the GDPR	76

Topic	*Answer*	*Paragraph(s) within the Farley judgment*
When claiming for non-material damage can a claimant claim only for distress?	The claimant can get compensation for: • distress; or • fear of consequences, resulting from the data breach.	75, 80
Can a person claim for annoyance or irritation?	Potentially, provided annoyance or irritation comes from a fear of third-party use of the data	93
What is the test for claiming for fear of the consequences of a breach?	Do the fears pass an 'objective standard of reasonableness' test, ie, is the fear well founded?	78
What would not pass this test?	Fleeting or transient subjective reactions unlikely to be enough	95
Myth busting – *Farley* opens the floodgates?	*Farley* relaxes some of the rules on compensation claims: • Damages can be awarded for annoyance or irritation. • However, the claimant must prove these, they cannot be hypothetical.	78, 93

Facts

2.23 The 432 claimants were police officers. They were members of a pension scheme administered by the defendant. Their annual pension statements were mistakenly posted to addresses that were wrong because they were out of date. Sussex Police had provided Paymaster with up-to-date addresses. The statements set out personal information including the officer's date of birth, national insurance number, and pension-related details including the officer's police service, salary details, and pension details. The police officers alleged that this was a misuse of their personal information and an infringement of the GDPR. Fourteen of the police officers could show an arguable case that the misaddressed envelope and been opened and that their statements had been read.[8] Some of the envelopes were not opened.

8 *Farley v Paymaster*, paras 1–5.

Cause of Action

2.24 The police officers brought a collective action seeking compensation for injury to feelings, and in some cases psychiatric injury, fearing that persons might misuse their data. [9]

Court findings

Disclosure of the data to a third party is not required for infringement of the GDPR

2.25 The defendant's action in printing the pension statement and placing it into an envelope constituted processing of the claimants' data for the purposes of the GDPR.

'Proof that the data were disclosed is not an essential ingredient of an allegation of processing or infringement.'[10]

The fact that some defendants' envelopes were not opened was not a bar to them receiving compensation.

Distress is not a pre-requisite for a claim

2.26 The court said 'An allegation of "distress" is not … an essential ingredient of a tenable claim.'[11]

Is there a threshold of seriousness in GDPR compensation claims?

2.27 Crucially, the Court of Appeal decided there is no threshold of seriousness in GDPR compensation claims.

The court said that the claims cannot be 'dismissed for failing to meet a threshold of seriousness. There is no such threshold in EU data protection law. We are not bound to hold that such a threshold exists in domestic data protection law. Nor is there any other good reason to do so.'[12]

However, there is a threshold of seriousness in misuse of private information claims (as the Court of Appeal said in *Prismall v Google* – see **Chapter 9**).

The claimant must show loss or damage if they are to receive compensation

2.28 The court made the point that mere infringement of the GDPR does not of itself allow for compensation. The claimant must also prove that damage was suffered.

9 *Ibid*, para 1.
10 *Ibid*, para 6.
11 *Ibid*, para 6.
12 *Ibid*, para 76.

The court said: 'The respondent is however entitled to contend that the appellants' fears of third-party misuse were not "well-founded" and hence cannot qualify as "non-material damage" for which compensation is recoverable under the GDPR … But the question must be answered case by case.'[13]

For a claimant to succeed, the must show infringement of the GDPR, as well as loss or damage being caused by the defendant's breach.

UK Court of Appeal followed the CJEU approach

2.29 The court referred to the Austrian post case from the Court of Justice of the European Union (CJEU) in 2023 and said:

> In all these circumstances I do not see any sufficiently weighty reason for departing on this appeal from the settled CJEU jurisprudence on the threshold of seriousness issue. It follows that there is no need to consider whether the individual claims would cross such a threshold.[14]

Distress is not a pre-requisite for a GDPR claim to succeed

2.30 The court said that they could rule out the 'contention that "distress" is an essential ingredient of a viable claim but also the respondent's alternative submission that the appellants' claims should be dismissed as falling short of a threshold of seriousness.'[15]

When claiming for non-material damage we know that a claimant can claim for distress. Can the claimant claim for irritation or annoyance?

2.31 In *Farley*, Lord Justice Warby said:

> A claim to be compensated for annoyance or irritation caused by fear of third-party misuse is tenable, provided the fear is well-founded. The CJEU jurisprudence tells us that such complaints cannot be dismissed for falling short of a threshold of seriousness.[16]

Hypothetical fears are not enough

2.32 The court in *Farley* referred to *VB* and *BL* (two CJEU cases) which said 'A purely hypothetical risk of misuse by an unauthorised third party cannot give rise to compensation.'[17]

13 *Ibid*, para 6
14 *Ibid*, paras 75 and 76.
15 *Ibid*, para 60.
16 *Ibid*, para 93.
17 *Ibid*, para 74.

Lords Justice Warby says 'in principle a claimant can recover compensation for fear of the consequences of an infringement if the alleged fear is objectively well-founded but not if the fear is (for instance) purely hypothetical or speculative.'[18]

So, the court is deciding whether a claimant's fear is objectively well-founded. What test does the court apply?

Objective standard

2.33 Lord Justice Warby said he would 'take the language used by the Court in VB and BL (two CJEU cases) to import an objective standard or test of reasonableness.'[19]

A person can obtain compensation if they have a well-founded fear

2.34 Lord Justice Warby went on to say:

> The test of reasonableness cannot depend on hindsight. It must be applied with reference to the facts and matters that were or should have been known to the appellant at the time they experienced the stated fear. That is implicit in paragraph [85] of VB and clearly correct in principle. It is obvious that a person can hold well-founded fears about future harm even if no such harm in fact results. If an illustration were needed, the facts of *George v Cannell* [2024] UKSC 19, [2024] 3 WLR 153 provide one.[20]

Fleeting reactions are not enough to being a successful GDPR claim

2.35 Lord Justice Warby said 'I would add that it seems to me there may be room for the view that fleeting or transient subjective reactions of this nature do not qualify as "non-material damage"'.[21]

What about the pleadings and the evidence?

If a claimant is claiming a 'well-founded fear' as a result of their data being lost, then the pleadings must reflect that

2.36 At para 84 of the judgment the court says that generic allegations in the pleadings would not be enough to provide the objective foundation for alleged fears because of a data breach. The court said that individual schedules would be required to prove the fear was well-founded. The court said that these individual schedules would need to set out the particular circumstances setting out a reasonable basis for the fear.

18 *Ibid*, para 75.
19 *Ibid*, para 78.
20 *Ibid*, para 80.
21 *Ibid*, para 95.

Does the UK still follow CJEU decisions?

2.37 The UK courts are not bound by the decisions of the CJEU.

The court in *Farley* said:

> We are bound by principles laid down by the CJEU and decisions made by it before IP Completion Day (the end of the Brexit implementation period on 31 December 2020). These are 'assimilated EU case law'. However, we are not bound by any principles laid down, or any decisions made, by the CJEU after that date; we 'may have regard' to such principles or decisions 'so far as it is relevant to any matter before the court'. In deciding how to approach the latter class of CJEU decisions we are of course bound by the domestic law of precedent.[22]

Permission to appeal the *Farley* case was granted on 17 December 2025 and the case will be heard in the Supreme Court.[23]

Does Farley open the floodgates?

2.38 *Farley* contained some good news for claimants.

The court says that a claimant can potentially be compensated for:

- fear of the consequences of a data breach; or
- other emotions such as anxiety or irritation as a result of the fear arising out of that breach.

However, these fears must be *objectively well founded* which means that claimants must be able to pass an objective standard of reasonableness test that they actually suffered these negative emotions.

TAKEAWAYS

2.39

- **Claim all applicable loss** – Ensure claimants have claimed all the damages to which they are entitled to, whether they are material (such as economic loss) or non-material (such as distress).
- **Pleadings** – Pleadings must be specific. Generic pleadings will not be enough especially where a claimant is claiming they suffered fear or apprehension because of a data breach. If a claimant is claiming such a fear, then the pleadings require individual schedules for each claimant setting out the nature of that fear or anxiety.

22 *Ibid*, para 30.
23 https://www.supremecourt.uk/cases/uksc-2025-0185.

- **Full and effective** – Claimants should ensure that the court and the defendants are aware that the GDPR says that compensation must be 'full end effective' and not derisory.
- **Other remedies include stopping processing the data** – As well as damages, a court can issue a compliance order requiring a controller or processor to take specific actions to comply with data protection law, such as ordering them to erase or grant access to data (see DPA 1998, s 167).

CHAPTER 3

Quantum in Data Protection Cases

INTRODUCTION

3.01 In previous chapters we assessed how damages in data protection cases were assessed under the statutory framework within Article 82 of the GDPR.

In this chapter we consider the level of damages awarded in UK data protection case law.

There is limited case law on data protection. We do know that many data protection claims settle before they reach court. Also, as many of them are heard in the county court, the court judgments often go unreported.

These cases serve as a useful guide to judicial trends on quantum in data protection compensation claims. Whilst there is much talk about the legal theory behind the assessment of damages, these cases are useful in helping us address how the damages were assessed in practice. Claimant and defence lawyers will find helpful information in the reported judgments below.

Whilst the author has considered some of these cases in other parts of the book, in this chapter we look at the cases through a different lens, specifically:

- the level of damages awarded; and
- the logic behind those awards.

PART I
MYTH BUSTING

3.02

- **Myth 1** – Claimants are routinely awarded large sums in data protection cases. This is incorrect. Awards in data protection claims are usually modest. Some cases have been in the £10,000–£20,000 range.
- **Myth 2** – Damages in data protection claims can be estimated with precision. This is also incorrect. The level of compensation awarded in data protection claims is messy and complicated. Many cases (such as *Reid v Price* below) have numerous intertwined factual issues and multiple causes of action. Many of the cases are fact- and context-specific. As the court in *Driver v CPS* said, setting damages in these cases is 'not an exact science'. Sometimes the case law can seem inconsistent. For example, in *Bekoe v Islington Borough Council*, a claimant received £6,000 when his financial information was unlawfully processed. In *Driver v CPS* the claimant received £250 when his information was unlawfully processed.

DAMAGES SUMMARY TABLE

3.03 Summary table on awards

Case	*Judgment available at*	*Year*	*Court*	*Defendant breaches*	*One-sentence summary*	*Award*
1. *ST (A Child) v L Primary School*	https://uk.practicallaw.thomsonreuters.com/D-104-8885?transitionType=Default&contextData=(sc.Default)	2020	High Court	• Data Protection Act (DPA 1998) • Article 8 right to privacy under the Human Rights Act 1998 (A8) • Misuse of private information (MOPI)	Child exhibited challenging behaviour at school – teacher wrote to other parents disclosing child's medical condition	Child –£1,500 Mother –£3,000
2. *Bekoe v London Borough of Islington*	https://www.bailii.org/ew/cases/EWHC/KB/2023/1668.html	2023	High Court	• Breach of GDPR • MOPI	Defendant local council unlawfully accessed claimant's information when preparing for a court claim	£6,000
3. *TLT & Ors v The Home Office*	https://www.bailii.org/ew/cases/EWHC/QB/2016/2217.html	2016	High Court	• A8	Claimants' names accidentally published on Home Office website as people with no right to remain in UK – claimants feared for their safety	£12,500

Case	*Judgment available at*	*Year*	*Court*	*Defendant breaches*	*One-sentence summary*	*Award*
4. *Driver v CPS*	https://www.bailii.org/ew/cases/EWHC/KB/2022/2500.html	2022	High Court	• Breach of GDPR • MOPI and A8 dismissed	CPS sent email to member of public containing data about claimant and an investigation about him – held to be unlawful processing with claimant suffering modest distress	£250
5. *Ali v Chief Con. Bedfordshire Police*	https://www.bailii.org/ew/cases/EWHC/KB/2023/938.html	2023	High Court	• GDPR • MOPI • Breach of confidence (BOC) • A8	Claimant made confidential report of ex-husband to police, employee of social services told the ex-husband of claimant's report causing distress to claimant	£3,000
6. *Wooley v Akram*	See here for an article on the case: https://www.pinsentmasons.com/out-law/news/scottish-court-issues-damages-to-couple-over-distress-caused-by-neighbours-use-of-cctv	2017	Scottish Sheriff Court	• DPA 1998	Neighbours carrying out surveillance of claimants with CCTV and audio for 2.5 years	£17,368

Case	*Judgment available at*	*Year*	*Court*	*Defendant breaches*	*One-sentence summary*	*Award*
7. *Aven & others*	https://www.5rb.com/wp-content/uploads/2020/09/Aven-Ors-v-Orbis-Business-Intelligence-Ltd-2020-EWHC-1812-QB.pdf	2020	High Court	• DPA 1998 • Multiple remedies sought, including a declaration and an order that the data be corrected	Claimants were businessmen – inaccurate and damaging information published about them	£18,000
8. *AB v MOJ*	https://www.bailii.org/ew/cases/EWHC/QB/2014/1965.html	2014	High Court	• DPA 1998	Claimant made data access request relating to material about coroner's proceedings and his late wife – defendant did not comply with the rules on data subject access requests	£2,250
9. *Reid v Katie Price*	https://www.bailii.org/ew/cases/EWHC/QB/2020/594.html	2020	High Court	• DPA 1998 • MOPI • BOC	Parties were divorced famous couple – defendant shared video and photo of claimant in sexual activity	£25,000

Case	*Judgment available at*	*Year*	*Court*	*Defendant breaches*	*One-sentence summary*	*Award*
10. *Brown v Police Commissioner*	https://uk.practicallaw.thomsonreuters.com/w-003-9258?transitionType=Default&contextData=(sc.Default)	2016	County Court	• DPA 1998 • A8	Claimant was police officer who went on holiday in breach of disciplinary rules – police sought information on her movements from border authority	£9,000
11. *Halliday v CCF*	https://www.bailii.org/ew/cases/EWCA/Civ/2013/333.html	2013	High Court	• DPA 1998	Defendant wrongly sent incorrect data to credit reference agency that claimant owed debt	£750

PART 2
THE CASES IN DETAIL

Case: *ST (A Child) v L Primary School* [2020] EWHC 1046 (QB)

3.04 **Court**: High Court

Date of judgment: 30 April 2020

Cause of action: Breach of the Data Protection Act 1998 (DPA 1998), ECHR Article 8 right to privacy, ECHR right against discrimination, MOPI.[1]

Facts:

- In this case, the headmaster of a school released details about a child's medical condition without the consent of the child's mother. The details appeared in a letter which was sent to the parents of other children in the school.
- The child in question would sometimes display challenging behaviour.[2]
- The headteacher sent the letter to all 60 parents of the school praising the child but mentioning that she had a condition which he said explained her behaviour.[3]
- The parent of the child did not consent to the letter being sent.
- Sending the letter breached the first data protection principle on fairness.
- None of the conditions for processing sensitive personal data were reached.[4]
- The child's Article 8 right to privacy was also breached by sending the information to people she did not know.
- The letter would not have been sent if the child was not disabled; hence the breach of her Article 14 rights (right against discrimination).[5]
- The letter was not justified or proportionate.
- The claimant's GDPR, misuse of private information, breach of Articles 8 and 14 of the Human Rights Act 1998 claims were successful.[6]

What the case says about damages:

- Double recovery in respect of various wrongs should be avoided – in other words, where there are two causes of action arising out of the same facts (in

1 *ST (A Child) v L Primary School*, para 1.
2 *Ibid*, para 8.
3 *Ibid*, paras 11 and 13.
4 *Ibid*, paras 68–72 and 75.
5 *Ibid*, para 100.
6 *Ibid*, para 120.

this case breach of the GDPR and MOPI), the claimants should only be able to recover once.[7]

- The child was awarded £1,500.[8]
- The parent would be awarded £3,000.

Case: *Bekoe v London Borough of Islington* [2023] EWHC 1668 (KB)

3.05 **Court**: High Court

Date of judgment: 5 July 2023

Cause of action: MOPI, Breach of claimant's GDPR rights[9]

Facts:

- In this case, a local council accessed information about a person's finances when it had no right to do so.
- The claimant had an elderly neighbour called Mrs S.
- Mrs S moved into a care home.
- The defendant, Islington Council, took possession proceedings for one of Mrs S's properties.
- The claimant challenged these proceedings as he believed he was given a right by Mrs S to manage her properties.
- Whilst preparing for the possession proceedings, the defendant council unfairly accessed financial information relating to the claimant to help it mount the possession proceedings.
- The claimant took proceedings for breach of the GDPR and was awarded compensation.[10]

What case says about damages:

- The defendant gave evidence as to the distress caused by the misuse of his information and the violation of his GDPR rights. The judge considered damages for both claims as a single figure.[11]
- The judge referred to the principles used in the *Gulati v MGN*[12] case, ie, that:
  - damages are compensatory not punitive;

7 *Ibid*, para 107.
8 *Ibid*, para 120
9 *Bekoe v London Borough of Islington*, para 1.
10 *Ibid*, paras 1–4.
11 *Ibid*, para 67.
12 *Gulati v MGN* [2015] EWHC 1482.

  - there are three aspects of conduct of the defendant which can trigger an aggravated damages awarded – the manner the wrong was committed, motive and subsequent conduct;
  - conduct can include the way the litigation is conducted by the defendant; and
  - a separate figure for aggravated damages can be given, or it can be wrapped up in the whole.[13]
- The judge felt the way that the trial and litigation had been conducted by the defendant revealed a lack of respect for legal requirements related to privacy and data protection.[14]
- In taking into account the:
  - MOPI;
  - the loss of the right to control information;
  - the level of distress caused by GDPR breaches; and
  - the aggravating factors,

  the court awarded an overall figure of £6,000.[15]

Case: *TLT & Ors v The Home Office* [2016] EWHC 2217 (QB)

3.06 **Court**: High Court

Date of judgment: 24 June 2016

Cause of action: Breach of GDPR, MOPI, breach of Article 8 rights

Facts:

- In this case, the Home Office in the UK caused a data breach. It released personal data about people who had no right to remain in the UK. This caused those people distress as they feared for their safety after having been 'outed' by the Home Office.
- The Home Office publishes quarterly statistics about the family returns process and how those with children who have no right to remain in the UK are returned to their country of origin.[16] The Home Office accidentally published personal data relating to individuals with no right to remain on the website.

13 *Bekoe v London Borough of Islington*, para 68.
14 *Ibid*, paras 68–69.
15 *Ibid*, paras 71–73.
16 *TLT & Ors v The Home Office*, para 1.

- It was discovered 13 days later and taken down.[17]
- The affected individuals were notified in January 2014.[18]
- The Home Office admitted a breach of the DPA 1998 as well as breach of confidence and MOPI.
- TLT was a citizen of Iran. He arrived in the UK on a visitor's visa, together with his wife, TLU, his then 17-year-old son and his daughter, TLV (aged 16), in 2010.[19]
- The court was impressed with the evidence of the claimants:
  - TLT was thought to be a calm, intelligent and straightforward witness;
  - TLU was said to be intelligent and thoughtful;[20] and
  - their daughter, TLV, was described as a bright and palpably honest young woman.
- Due to concerns about their information being in the public domain, TLT and TLU relocated from the area in which they lived and moved to a new area.
- TLT and TLU genuinely believed their security was compromised and feared for their own safety.[21]

What case says about damages:

- In the cases of TLT and TLU, their circumstances and the 'distress' which they experienced were comparable and should result in an identical award. The court assessed damages in each of their cases at £12,500. This is not out of kilter with awards for moderate psychiatric and psychological damage.[22]
- The case of TLV was different. She was protected by her youth and by the care which her parents took to shield her from knowledge of what was happening.[23]
- Nevertheless, TLV too experienced genuine concern, in particular about her family in Iran, and did have her schooling and friendships disrupted. In her case, the court assessed damages at £2,500.[24]

Case: *Driver v CPS* [2022] EWHC 2500 (KB)

3.07 **Court**: High Court

17 *Ibid*, paras 2, 3, 4.
18 *Ibid*, para 6.
19 *Ibid*, para 21.
20 *TLT & Ors v The Home Office*, para 23.
21 *Ibid*, para 28.
22 *Ibid*, para 29.
23 *Ibid*, para 30.
24 *Ibid*, paras 29, 30.

Date of judgment: 10 October 2022

Cause of action: Breach of GDPR succeeded, MOPI, breach of the Human Rights Act 1998 (HRA 1998) failed.

Facts:

- The claimant was a local politician. He was a suspect in a criminal investigation.
- A member of the public asked the Crown Prosecution Service (CPS) for details about the investigation and the CPS obliged.
- The CPS had already released a statement about the investigation. The court found that the person should not have received an update about the investigation.
- The claimant claimed breach of the GDPR and/or the Data Protection Act (DPA 2018) because it constituted the unlawful processing of his personal data.[25]
- The court found that the person should not have received an update about the investigation and that this update was a breach of the claimant's data protection rights.

Breaches[26]

- The court found there was a breach of the first (fair and lawful), second (purpose limitation) and sixth (security) data protection principles under the GDPR.[27]
- The court accepted that it can be a legitimate function of the police and the CPS to keep the public at large updated about how far enquiries have reached. But in this case there had been public statements to the media which fully and appropriately briefed the public on the matter. Unless and until a charging decision was taken, there was no pressing social need for anything further to be said.
- The court concluded that the disclosure to the member of the public about the case was not necessary.[28]
- The court concluded that there was a breach of the sixth data protection (security) principle. The CPS has failed to show that it had in place appropriate organisational measures to protect against unauthorised or unlawful processing.
- The MOPI claim was dismissed[29] as was the HRA 1998 claim.[30]

25 *Driver v CPS*, para 2.
26 *Ibid*, paras 119–121.
27 *Ibid*, paras 119–121.
28 *Ibid*, para 121.
29 *Ibid*, para 160).
30 *Ibid*, para 165.

What case says about damages:

- The court agreed that 'there were few reported cases on quantum for breaches of data protection legislation, and that assessing damages in this area was 'not an exact science'.[31]
- The judge said that the 'Claimant would have experienced a very modest degree of distress upon discovering that the CPS's email had been sent to political opponents and the media by someone who had a grievance against him in an effort (as I find) to embarrass him.'[32]
- The judge further said that 'I consider that this data breach was at the lowest end of the spectrum. Taking all matters together in the round, I award the Claimant damages of £250. I will also make a declaration that the Defendant breached the Claimant's rights under Part 3 of the DPA 2018'.[33]

Case: *Ali v Chief Constable of Bedfordshire Police* [2023] EWHC 938 (KB)

3.08 **Court**: High Court (KB)

Date of judgment: 25 Apri 2023

Cause of action: Breach of GDPR, MOPI, breach of confidence, breach of Article 8 right to privacy all succeeded.[34]

Facts:

- In this case, the claimant had confidentially reported her ex-husband to the police as she suspected he was dealing drugs.
- The claimant wanted action to be taken against him and said that she believed he posed a risk to her and her children.
- The claimant made very clear that she did not want to be identified as the source of the information.
- She met a police officer, who made a report, which recorded that she was 'frightened of repercussions from speaking to the police'.
- The report was passed on to the Social Services Department of Luton Borough Council (department).

31 *Ibid*, para 166.
32 *Ibid*, para 168.
33 *Ibid*, para 169.
34 *Ali v Chief Constable of Bedfordshire Police*, para 3.

- An employee of that department who happened to be in a relationship with Ms Ali's ex-husband unlawfully accessed and downloaded a copy of the report and passed it to the ex-husband.[35]
- The claimant said numerous times that she did not want to be identified.[36]
- The court said 'The key issue in this case is whether the disclosure by the Police of Ms Ali's identity as the source of the information was "necessary" for one of the purposes identified in Article 6(1) of the GDPR ... In my judgment, the Police have failed to carry that burden in this case.'[37]
- The claimant had also been assured that her anonymity would be preserved.
- The police breached the fair and lawful processing principle under the GDPR as well as the purpose limitation principle.[38]

What the case says about damages:

- The court found the claimant was entitled to some compensation for distress under the GDPR.
- The court found that the appropriate sum was £3,000. It noted that this was in the bottom half of the range of awards for 'less severe psychiatric harm' in the Judicial College Guidelines for the Assessment of General Damages in Personal Injury Cases (16th edn).[39]
- The claims for GDPR misuse of private information and breach of section 6 of the HRA 1998 all succeeded.[40]

Case: *Anthony Woolley and Deborah Woolley v Nahib Akbar Or Akram* [2017] SC EDIN 7, 3 February 2017

3.09 **Court**: Scottish Sheriff Court

Date of judgment: February 2017

Cause of action: Breach of the first (fair and lawful principle), third (data minimisation principle) and fifth data protection principle (security principle) under the DPA 1998.

Facts:

- In this case, the defender spied on the pursuers who were their neighbours. They recorded them on CCTV for 2.5 years.

35 *Ibid*, para 1.
36 *Ibid*, para 31.
37 *Ibid*, paras 27–30.
38 *Ibid*, para 37.
39 *Ibid*, para 52.
40 *Ibid*, para 55.

- The pursuers lived above a guest house which was owned by the defender.
- The guest house was proposed as a bail hostel.
- The relationship between the parties broke down.
- The defender installed security cameras and audio recording devices which were highly intrusive. They recorded 24 hours per day.
- The defender said the security cameras were in place to record any confrontation between the parties. They deliberately covered the pursuers property.
- The court found that the defender was in breach of:
  - the first data protection principle – fair and lawful processing;
  - the third data protection principle – adequacy, relevance and proportionality; and
  - the fifth data protection principle – storage limitation.

What the case says about damages:

- The court awarded £17,268 in compensation under section 31(1) of the DPA 1998 for distress caused by the intrusive CCTV and audio recording at the family home.
- Sheriff Ross accepted the Wooley's claim for damages which was for £10 daily for a period of 2.5 years awarding them £8,634 each, totalling £17,268.
- The Woolley's suffered considerable distress given the infringement of their privacy.
- The court said that the amount awarded was a 'modest and reasonable assessment' in the circumstances.[41]

Case: *Aven and Others v Orbis Business Intelligence Ltd* [2020] EWHC 1812 (QB)

3.10 **Court**: High Court (QB)

Date of judgment: 8 July 2020

Cause of action: The claimant sought four remedies:

- a declaration that the personal data were inaccurate and in breach of the fair and lawful principle;[42]
- an order for:

41 *Woolley v Akram* – Case Digest, Practical Law, Thomson Reuters.
42 *Aven and Others v Orbis Business Intelligence Limited*, para 8.

- blocking;
- erasure;
- destruction; and
- rectification of the personal data;

- an order that the defendant inform those to whom it disclosed such inaccuracies; and
- compensation.[43]

The claimants were successful on all these grounds.

Facts:

- The claimants were three businessmen of Russian or Ukrainian origin.
- The defendant was a consultancy group, Orbis, providing investigative services to clients. On the instructions of a Washington DC consultancy in 2016, it was asked to produce a report on the claimants and provide intelligence memoranda concerning any links which might exist between Russia, its president, Vladimir Putin, and Donald Trump.
- The defendant produced a report on the claimants, the so-called 'Steele Dossier'.
- Buzz feed news published articles referring to the dossiers in 2017.[44]
- The claimants said the information in the report was inaccurate[45] and sought correction of the report and other remedies.
- The court said that 'The claimants have discharged the burden of proving that the data are inaccurate or misleading as a matter of fact.'[46]

What did court find?

- The court found that the defendant did breach the accuracy principle under the DPA 1998.
- The court granted a limited order for rectification in respect of all the inaccurate data and awarded £18,000 compensation to each of the first and second claimants.[47]
- There was limited discussion about how the compensation figure was calculated.

43 *Ibid*, para 8.
44 *Ibid*, paras 1–4.
45 *Ibid*, para 8.
46 *Ibid*, para 204.
47 *Ibid*, para 204.

Case: *AB v Ministry of Justice* [2014] EWHC 1847 (QB)

3.11 **Court**: High Court (QB)

Date of judgment: 11 June 2014

Cause of action: breach of the defendant's duty under section 7 of the DPA 1998. Successful.

Facts:

- The claimant was a prominent solicitor in practice for many years.
- The claimant made a data subject access request (DSAR) in September 2007, seeking his personal data including material relating to the coroner's proceedings concerning his late wife.
- The claimant received only a partial response to his DSAR in April 2009. This was more than 18 months after he made the DSAR.[48]
- Baker J found that 'The defendant has contravened the provisions of the DPA 1998 in relation to the provision of the disclosed material, and one item of the withheld material. The contravention in relation to the former material being a delay in its provision for a period of something less than 17 months, and in relation to the latter material a delay in its provision for a period of over 6 years'.[49]

What the case says about damages:

- In terms of damages: 'Although I am satisfied that he has suffered damage in accordance with s.13(1) of the DPA 1998, I consider that this is a case in which an award of nominal damages is appropriate under this head, which will be in the conventional sum of £1.00.'[50]
- The claimant was found to have suffered some distress as a result of the delays in dealing with his DSAR.
- Baker J said: 'I have no medical evidence before me. Therefore, doing the best I am able to on the evidence before me I consider that any award of compensation for distress caused as a result of the relevant delays in this case, should be in the sum of £2,250.00.'[51]

48 *Ibid*, para 18.
49 *Ibid*, para 55.
50 *Ibid*, paras 55–56.
51 *Ibid*, para 57.

Case: *Alexander Reid v Katie Price* [2020] EWHC 594 (QB)

3.12 **Court**: High Court (QB) Media and Communications List

Date of judgment: 13 March 2020

Cause of action: damages for breach of confidence, MOPI and breach of contract, and compensation under the DPA 1998. The breach of contract claim did not succeed.

Facts:

- In this case, Katie Price, the glamour model, shared sexual videos of her ex-husband.
- The claimant and the defendant are both celebrities. He is a martial artist, known as a 'cage fighter', who appeared on and won the TV series Big Brother.
- She is a former 'glamour' model, who is also known by the stage name 'Jordan'.
- In or about 2009, the claimant and defendant became a couple. On 2 February 2010, they were married. The relationship foundered within about a year, and a divorce was finalised on 20 March 2012.[52]
- During the relationship, in October 2009 and June 2010, the defendant obtained video recordings and photographs of the claimant engaged in sexual activity.[53]
- He claimed that on a number of occasions in and between about 2012 and 9 January 2018, the defendant disclosed all or part of the private information to third parties, numbering at least 50.
- He also complained that she had breached the undertakings (that she had previously given not to disclose certain information) by publicly describing one aspect of the private information.[54]
- At the *relevant* hearing, the claimant was present and represented but the defendant was not present or represented.
- The claimant says he was 'absolutely horrified' when he realised in 2013 that the defendant was holding on to the footage of him.
- He found the repeated references to his sex life in the media 'very demeaning and harassing'. He had been mocked and denigrated as a sexual deviant and predator.

52 *Alexander Reid v Katie Price*, para 1.
53 *Ibid*, para 3.
54 *Ibid*, para 4.

- He sought counselling for stress and anxiety, which he attributed to the defendant's disclosures. He saw a number of psychologists and a hypnotherapist.
- He also sought therapy concerning his low self-esteem.[55]
- The claimant established a claim based on four different causes of action.
- The court found that it did not consider that the contract claim added anything of relevance.
- The court did not see any material difference between the approach to be taken to the claims in confidentiality, MOPI, and breach of statutory duty.
- The essential task was to compensate the claimant for the wrongful retention and wrongful disclosure of images of his sexual conduct, and the wrongful disclosure of information about that conduct.[56]

What the case says about damages:

- 'Compensation for the tortious disclosure of personal information should aim to restore the claimant to the position he would have occupied but for the tort … damages may include compensation for distress, hurt feelings and loss of dignity; it may also be appropriate to take into account any aggravating conduct by the defendant which increases the hurt to the claimant's feelings; damages should be proportionate, they should not be open to criticism for arbitrariness; but they must be adequate to mark the wrong and provide a measure of solatium'.[57]
- The court was satisfied that this claim merited £25,000 in damages.[58]
- The court accepted that the defendant's conduct involved the deliberate exposure to a substantial number of individuals of moving and still images of the claimant's intimate sexual activity, which were taken without his consent and disclosed in the knowledge that he positively objected.
- The court found that the defendant's conduct had considerably aggravated the harm caused by the disclosures themselves.
- Th court found that the defendant's behaviour had been persistent, flagrant, arrogant, high-handed, and inexcusable, and for those reasons very distressing and hurtful to the claimant.[59]
- The court found that: 'The defendant's frequent additional references or allusions to the Private Information, sometimes in threatening terms, have caused additional upset, "rubbing salt in the wound". Damages of £25,000 would be comparable to an award for moderately severe psychiatric harm, or a neck injury leaving markedly impaired function. Applying the principles

55 *Ibid*, para 47.
56 *Ibid*, para 49.
57 *Ibid*, para 50.
58 *Ibid*, para 54.
59 *Ibid*, para 60.

I have identified above, an award at that level or more is fully merited, on any view of the authorities'.[60]

Case: *Andrea Brown v Commissioner or Police of the Metropolis* Claim Number 3YM09078

3.13 **Court**: County Court

Date of judgment: 7 October 2016

Cause of action: breach of the DPA 1998 and breach of the HRA 1998 – both successful.

Facts:

- In this case, the claimant was a police officer. She was off on sick leave. She went to Barbados on holiday without telling her manager.
- As part of the disciplinary process, a police officer from the claimant's employer submitted a request for information on her to the National Border Targeting Centre which had information about travellers to and from the UK.[61]
- The question was whether the police had gone too far in asking the border authority for data about the claimant's travels.
- The claimant argued that the data facilities at the border authority are for police to use in detection of crime and that the police had therefore processed her data in an excessive way.[62]
- The defendant admitted liability.[63]
- The court considered remedies for breach of the DPA 1998 and the HRA 1998 and tortious interference with the right to privacy.[64]
- The claimant sought aggravated damages.

What the case says about damages:

- The court said 'doing the best I can, I fix the global sum of damages at £9,000. I believe that reflects the distress experienced by the claimant and compensates the extent to which she ceased to be in control of her perianal information.'[65]

60 *Ibid*, para 60.
61 *Andrea Brown v Commissioner or Police of the Metropolis*, para 6.
62 *Ibid*, para 14.
63 *Ibid*, para 17.
64 *Ibid*, para 20.
65 *Ibid*, para 75.

Case: *Halliday v Creation Consumer Finance* [2013] EWCA Civ 333

3.14 **Court**: Court of Appeal

Date of judgment: 15 March 2013

Cause of action: breach of the DPA 1998 – successful.

- The claimant had purchased a television set and, when he did so, he entered into a credit agreement with the defendant, Creation Consumer Finance (CCF).
- In earlier and unrelated court proceedings, the defendant agreed to pay the claimant £1,500.
- As part of those earlier proceedings, CCF agreed to delete all data relating to Mr Halliday and to provide him with a list of any third parties to whom it released his data to.
- However, CCF then made a mistake. It made incorrect data entries on its system and forwarded its data to a credit referencing agency called Equifax.
- Equifax then produced a report based on this incorrect information which showed the claimant as owing money. Mr Halliday was undoubtedly very concerned to discover this.
- The court said: 'there was wrongful processing of Mr Halliday's data, but the object of the award … is to compensate, neither more nor less. The breach was … of a limited nature. It did not lead to loss of creditor reputation. Likewise there is no proof of any fraudulent or malicious intent on the part of CCF … this breach was … a single episode case. There was one error. It has been explained how it occurred.

  There is, in addition, no contemporary evidence of any manifestation of injury to feelings and distress apart from what one would normally expect from frustration at these prolonged and protracted events … the sum to be awarded should be of a relatively modest nature since it is not the intention of the legislation to produce some kind of substantial award. It is intended to be compensation, and thus I would consider it sufficient to render an award in the sum of £750. It seems to me that that sum is appropriate and sufficient.'[66]
- The Court of Appeal said the claimant's frustration necessitated an award of £750.[67]

66 *Halliday v Creation Consumer Finance*, paras 33–36.
67 *Ibid*, paras 13–17 and 49.

TAKEAWAYS

3.15

(1) **Aggravated damages** – There are three aspects of conduct of the defendant which can trigger an aggravated damages awarded – the manner the wrong was committed, motive and subsequent conduct (see *Bekoe v London Borough of Islington*).

(2) **Double recovery** – Where multiple causes of actions arise out of the same facts then the courts have shown an aversion to 'double recovery'. The court said in *ST (A Child) v L Primary School* that 'double recovery in respect of various wrongs should be avoided'.

(3) **Is the claimant an impressive witness?** – In some of the cases, for example *TLT v Home Office*, the court was obviously impressed with the strength of the claimant's evidence. The claimants were able to show the impact the data breach had caused. They received substantial damages as a result. Whilst this may seem an obvious point, much will turn on whether the claimant is a compelling witness. Claimant lawyers should assess the strength of the claimant's evidence when trying to value the claim in advance of a hearing.

CHAPTER 4

Costs and Case Management

INTRODUCTION

4.01 The costs rules in the UK help promote proportionality and settlement when it comes to UK data protection litigation.

This chapter comprises three parts which deal with:

- the principles for issuing a data protection claim in the correct court;
- the costs rules; and
- risks in respect of costs in data protection claims and how they can be mitigated.

PART I
WHICH COURT?[1]

4.02 The summary table below sets out an overview of the rules on selecting the appropriate court in a data protection claim.

Which court?		
Topic	**In a nutshell**	**In practice**
1. County court or High Court?	• Claims for less than £100k must be issued in the county court unless too complex	• Historically awards have been low in data protection claims • See CPR 7.A PD
2. Which list in the High Court?	• Data protection and misuse of private information (MOPI) cases should be started in the Media and Communications List	• See CPR 53
3. Small claims?	• Claims under £10k but only for simple data claims	• Data claims issued under the small claims track are often moved to the county court fast track or multi track

1 See Practice Direction 7A.

Basic Principles on Court Selection

4.03 Whether a case should be tried in the county court or the High Court is governed by Practice Direction 7A.

- Claims for less than £100,000 must be issued in the county court.[2]
- Personal injury claims of less than £50,000 must be issued in the county court.[3]

However, there are some exceptions to these thresholds. A claim may be issued in the High Court by reason of:

- the financial value of the claim;
- the complexity of the case; and
- the importance of the outcome of the claim to the public in general.[4]

Taking a Case to the High Court – Which List?

4.04 Where a case is taken on any of the following causes of actions:

- breach of data protection law;
- misuse of private information (MOPI); and
- defamation,

  and the case is taken to the High Court, then the case should be started in the Media and Communications List of the High Court (CPR 53.1).

I Have Decided to Issue my Data Protection Claim in the County Court. Is the Small Claims Track the Appropriate Track?

4.05 The small claims track is for simple, low-value claims.

Issuing a claim under the small claims track is the normal track for claims under £10,000 (see CPR 26.9 which sets out the scope of each track).

However, the small claims track is often not the most appropriate track for data protection claims because they often involve complex issues. For example, a case may involve a debate about the GDPR technical definitions. Under CPR 26.9 (4), the court office can reallocate the small claim to a different track. If a data claim is too complex for the small claims track, then usually the court will allocate it to

2 Practice Direction (PD) 7A.2.1.
3 Practice Direction (PD) 7A.2.2.
4 Practice Direction (PD) 7A.2.4.

another track within the county court. It may allocate the claim to the fast track if it is medium value or to the multi-track if it is complex or high value.

The small claims track will usually only work if there is a relatively simple breach of the GDPR.

Self-litigants – nothing to lose?

4.06 Small claims actions have almost no risk on costs for self-litigants. A self-litigant won't usually be liable for the defendant's costs even if they lose a case under the small claims track (unless they are found to have behaved unreasonably). This can be advantageous for the self-litigant because the costs asymmetry can put pressure on the defendant to pay the claimant off particularly in low-value 'nuisance' cases.

The author has seen some low-value claims settle early for this reason.

If a data protection case is allocated to any of the following tracks in the county court, then there will be costs implications, as follows:

- small claims track – costs recovery will be limited. If a claimant instigates an action in the small claims court, they won't usually recover their costs even if they win;
- fast track – costs are fixed (ie, the costs are fixed to set limits); and
- intermediate track – costs are fixed.

On the Wrong Track?

4.07 Many data protection claims have been criticised for being on the wrong track.

For example:

- *Rolfe & Others v Veale Wasbrough Vizards LLP*.[5] This minor missent email case was taken to the High Court. Master McCloud said 'In the modern world it is not appropriate for a party to claim, (especially in the in the High Court) for breaches of this sort'.[6]
- In *Johnson v Eastlight*[7] (a low-value claim where the claimant's data was sent to the wrong person), Master Thornet said:
  - 'I see no basis for this claim having been issued in the High Court ... CPR PD7A Para 2.1 is explicit: "Proceedings ... may not be

5 *Rolfe & Others v Veale Wasbrough Vizards LLP* [2021] EWHC 2809 (QB).
6 *Ibid*, para 13.
7 *Johnson v Eastlight* [2021] EWHC 3069 (QB).

started in the High Court unless the value of the claim is more than £100,000".'[8]

- 'Everything about this case has all of the hallmarks of a Small Claim Track claim that should have been issued in the County Court and so allocated. The suggestion that this is a developing area of law or where, even if principle is established, requires elaborate and complex legal argument is unrealistic if not, at least arguably, opportunistic.'[9]
- 'The presentation and processing of this case to-date in this forum has, I am satisfied, constituted a form of procedural abuse.'[10]

Claimant's must be made aware of the risks of issuing low-value claims in the High Court. Lawyers would be advised to take a clear-eyed view of costs.

PART 2
OVERVIEW ON COSTS

4.08 This summary table below sets out an overview of the rules on costs.

Overview of costs summary		
Topic	**In a nutshell**	**In practice**
• What are costs?	• Includes fees, charges, disbursements, expenses	• See CPR 44
• What discretion does the court have on costs?	Court has wide discretion on: • amount of costs • whether to disallow costs	• See CPR 44 2-11
• When might a court go against the 'loser pays' principle?	Court will consider all the circumstances, including: • conduct of the parties • whether admissible offers of settlements were made	• See CPR 44.4

In data cases, the amount of costs often is much greater than the amount awarded in damages as GDPR cases can often be low-value claims. For example, in the Naomi Campbell case,[11] the professional model took a case against the Mirror Group Newspapers for publishing photos of her attending a meeting relating to tackling her alleged drug addiction. Ms Campbell sued under the Data Protection Act 1998 and for breach of confidence. The supermodel was awarded £3,500

8 *Ibid*, para 24.1.
9 *Ibid*, para 24.5.
10 *Ibid*, para 24.3.
11 *Campbell v MGN Ltd* [2004] UKHL 22.

in damages and costs of £1,086,295.47 – not a good look for Mirror Group Newspapers.[12]

In this Part of the chapter, we will consider an overview of the costs rules in England in Wales.

What are the Main Rules on Costs and What do they Say?

4.09 The primary legislation which gives courts the power to award costs is set out at section 51(1) of the Senior Courts Act 1981. Courts can make orders for costs 'of and incidental to' proceedings.

'Incidental to' is something that is a live issue in data breach actions. For example, in *Weaver v British Airways* (see below), there was a debate about the extent to which a claimant's solicitor could seek £443,000 costs relating to advertising for claimants after there was a large-scale data breach. Ultimately these costs were disallowed.

The framework for costs in England and Wales is set out at CPR 44. These rules will be seen against the background of the overriding objective of the CPR rule which is to enable the court to deal with cases justly and at a proportionate cost.

Costs are defined in CRPR 44.1. The have a broad definition and include:

- fees, charges, disbursements (such as court fees, expert reports);
- expenses, remuneration (lawyers' fees); and
- costs for litigants in person.

There are further costs rules set out at CPR 45 (dealing with fixed costs), CPR 45 (dealing with costs in special cases including group litigation orders as well as wasted costs orders against lawyers) and CPR 46 (costs in special cases).

The Courts Discretion as to Costs

4.10 CPR 44.2(1) sets out that the court has discretion as to:

- whether costs are payable by one party to another;
- the amount of those costs; and
- when they are to be paid.

12 Richard Morgan and Ruth Boardman, *Data Protection Strategy*, Sweet & Maxwell, 3rd edn, p 72.

Costs Assessment Hearings

4.11 When an order for costs is made, the amount to be paid will be determined by an assessment process at court if it is not agreed by the parties.[13]

What Types of Costs Orders Can the Court Make?

4.12 Courts have a wide discretion in terms of the orders for costs that they can make.

CPR 44.2(6) says that a court has a wide scope for the types of costs orders that it can make in a case. It can make orders that a party must pay:

(a) a *proportion* of another party's costs;

(b) a *stated amount* in respect of another party's costs;

(c) costs from or *until a certain date* only;

(d) *costs incurred before proceedings* have begun;

(e) costs relating to *particular steps taken* in the proceedings;

(f) costs relating only to a distinct *part of the proceedings*; and

(g) *interest* on costs from or until a certain date, including a date before judgment.

The Golden Rule: Loser (Usually) Pays

4.13 CPR 44.2(2) sets out that if the court does decide to make an order for costs, then:

(a) the general rule is that the unsuccessful party will be ordered to pay the costs of the successful party; but

(b) the court may make a different order.

When Might a Court make a Different Order?

4.14 The court has wide powers to make a different order that goes against the loser pays principle.

CPR 44.4(3) sets out that in deciding what order of costs to make the court will consider all the circumstances, including the conduct of all the parties.

Assessing the conduct of the parties will include:

(a) *conduct* before, as well as during, the proceedings;

(b) the *efforts* made to try to resolve the dispute;

13 'Costs: An overview', Practical Law Dispute Resolution, Thomson Reuters.

(c) the amount or *value* of the claim;

(d) the *importance* of the matter to all the parties;

(e) the particular *complexity* of the matter or the difficulty or novelty of the questions raised;

(f) the *skill, effort, specialised knowledge* and responsibility involved;

(g) the *time spent* on the case; and

(h) the place where and the *circumstances* in which work or any part of it was done.[14]

The Nuclear Button – Courts' Powers in Relation to Misconduct

4.15 Under CPR Rule 44.11, the court can press the nuclear button and disallow all costs where:

- the conduct of a party or that party's legal representative
- either before or during the proceedings
- was unreasonable or improper.

PART 3
RISKS IN RESPECT OF COSTS IN DATA PROTECTION CLAIMS AND HOW THEY CAN BE MITIGATED

4.16 In this part of the chapter, we look at how some of the key risks on costs may arise in data protection claims and how they may be mitigated.

This summary table below sets out an overview of the risks relating to costs in data protection claims.

Risks on costs in data protection claims		
Risk	*In a nutshell*	*In practice*
1. Proportionality	• In deciding whether to award costs, the court will consider whether they are proportionate	• Many data claims end up with micro awards and huge costs bills – eg, *Campbell v MGN* where the award was £3k, and the costs were £1m • Courts can disallow costs if disproportionate • See CPR 44.4

14 CPR 44.4(3).

Risk	*In a nutshell*	*In practice*
2. Unreasonable conduct	• Courts can penalise a party on costs when they plead pointless heads of claim	• Claimants should avoid throwing multiple privacy-related causes of action at the wall in the hope that one of them will stick • See CPR 44.2(5)
3. Exaggerated claims	• Court will consider all the circumstances, including conduct of the parties	• Courts have criticised some claimants in data cases for exaggerated claims (eg, claiming anxiety in cases involving missent email and innocuous data) • See CPR 44.2(5)
4. Group claims	• The stakes are higher for group claims	• In *Weaver v BA* [2021] EWHC 217 (QB), the High Court said advertising costs were not recoverable • Some data group claims have failed leaving costs of millions of pounds • Group claims need a solid foundation (eg, BA data breach)
5. Settlements	• If a claimant refuses a Part 36 settlement offer which it then does not beat in court, it can be penalised on costs	• Data claims can be very unpredictable due to the complexity of the law; be careful in refusing reasonable settlement offers

RISK 1 – PROPORTIONALITY

4.17 If parties incur disproportionate costs, they can be penalised on costs.

What is proportionality in costs cases? The court may penalise a party who incurs unreasonable costs.

Proportionality is a key tenet to litigation in England and Wales. The overriding objective at Part 1 of the CPR Rules is to enable the court to deal with cases justly and at a proportionate cost.

What does the CPR say about Proportionality?

Factors to be considered in deciding the amount of costs

4.18 CPR 44.4 says the court will have regard to all the circumstances in deciding whether costs were proportionate and reasonable.

In making this assessment about proportionality, the court will assess numerous factors (in CPR 44.4(3)) including

- the amount or value of any money or property involved;
- the importance of the matter to all the parties;
- the skill, effort, specialised knowledge and responsibility involved; and
- the time spent on the case.

The court will consider whether the costs are proportionate and sensible taking into account the relevant factors in the case.

Why is Proportionality a Risk in GDPR Claims?

Low awards

4.19 Often breach of the GDPR can mean that a claimant suffers limited damages, such as distress or inconvenience.

Awards in GDPR cases have been historically low, for example, see *Driver v CPS.*[15] In that case, the claimant was a local politician. The Crown Prosecution Service sent an email to a member of the public containing his data.[16] The claimant claimed breach of the GDPR, MOPI, and breach of his Article 8 right to privacy. The High Court found that the email should not have been sent.[17] The claimant experienced a very modest degree of distress[18] and was only awarded £250. Whilst the claimant was not penalised on costs, this example underlines the potential for low awards in data claims which can pose a costs risk.

Claimant lawyers should be aware of the potential for low awards in data protection cases and they should avoid incurring disproportionate costs.

15 *Driver v CPS* [2022] EWHC 2500 (KB) – see https://www.bailii.org/ew/cases/EWHC/KB/2022/2500.html.
16 *Ibid*, para 2.
17 *Ibid*, paras 119–212.
18 *Ibid*, para 168.

Mitigation

4.20

- Keep the overring objective and need for proportionality front of mind.
- Whether acting for the claimant or defendant, lawyers should take a view at an early stage on what the maximum value of the case is.
- Keep account of how costs are mounting.
- Don't let the tail wag the dog (ie, avoid spending thousands of pounds on costs in low-value claims).
- Time is valuable resource too – wasting time on a tiny case in not in your client's interest.

RISK 2 – UNREASONABLE CONDUCT AND POINTLESS CAUSES OF ACTION

How is the Conduct of the Parties Relevant?

4.21 If parties behave unreasonably, they can be penalised on costs.

Parties must be careful in raising or disputing causes of actions when it is futile to do so.

CPR 44.2.4(a) says 'In deciding what order (if any) to make about costs, the court will have regard to all the circumstances, including – (a) the conduct of all the parties'.

The conduct of the parties is considered at CPR Article 44(2)(5) and includes whether it was reasonable for a party to raise, pursue or contest an issue and the way they did so.

Why is Unreasonable Conduct a Costs Risk in GDPR Claims?

4.22 The conduct of the parties often arises in data protection breach claims.

Data protection and privacy law is complex. This can lead to claimants hedging their bets when it comes to pleading causes of action. They often decide to 'throw the kitchen sink' at the case using the flawed logic that if one cause fails then they might get lucky on another. This can be risky from a cost perspective.

The author has experience of litigation where the defendants were in breach of not answering a claimant's GDPR data subject access request. The defendants had no defence to this. However, the defendants fought the case on very spurious grounds. They ultimately had to pay a much larger costs bill than if they had settled early.

What does the Case Law Say?

Claimant accused of 'procedural abuse'

4.23 In *Johnson v Eastlight Community Homes Ltd*[19]:

- The claimant was a tenant of a social housing provider.
- In 2020, the defendant accidentally emailed another tenant a document which included the claimant's name, email, and payment history.
- The recipient deleted the email within three hours.
- The claimant claimed for damages for MOPI, breach of confidence and negligence, together with damages for breach of Article 8 ECHR as well as damages pursuant to Article 82 GDPR and damages pursuant to section 169 of the DPA 2018.[20]
- The claimant claimed anxiety but not personal injury.[21]

Outcome

- The case was before the Master in the High Court.
- The MoPI, breach of confidence, and Article 8 claims were struck out and the GDPR claim was transferred to the county court (small claims track).
- The case was referred for a costs assessment hearing.[22]
- Master Thornett displayed an effective use of British understatement when he criticised the multiple causes of action in this claim. He said 'Despite an initial impression of sophistry, the Particulars of Claim ultimately comprises a number of overlapping and often inadequately pleaded causes of action.[23]
- With respect to procedural abuse, Master Thornett went on to say 'No serious privately paying litigant would contemplate spending over £50,000 in costs, not all of which may prove recoverable even in the event of success, and similarly expose themselves to the risk of a significant adverse costs order following High Court litigation if unsuccessful, for a damages claim less than £3,000. The presentation and processing of this case to-date in this

19 *Johnson v Eastlight Community Homes Ltd* [2021] EWHC 3069 (QB) – see https://www.bailii.org/ew/cases/EWHC/QB/2021/3069.html.
20 *Ibid*, paras 1–3.
21 *Ibid*, paras 4-6.
22 *Ibid*, para 24.
23 *Ibid*, para 23.

forum has, I am satisfied, constituted a form of procedural abuse … I am satisfied that the real point in this case is whether the Claimant's entitlement is to purely nominal or instead extremely low damages.'[24]

- The Master then asked the parties to agree costs amongst themselves based upon his comments.[25]

Claimant rebuked

4.24 In *Stadler v Currys Group Ltd*[26] Judge Lewis was not complimentary about the way in which costs were incurred in the case and said:

> By including multiple causes of action in respect of this low value claim, the claimant has increased the complexity of the proceedings unnecessarily … The claimant's costs in respect of these applications are close to £11,000. This needs to be considered in the context of a claim that might end up being worth just a few hundred pounds.[27]

How to Mitigate this Risk?

Claimants

4.25 Pleading the right cause of action is not easy. Lawyers would be advised to do the hard thinking right at the start of proceedings and to obtain counsel's opinion on the merits of the claim. This can help prevent:

- wasting resource on pointless causes of action that won't succeed; and
- losing the sympathy and credibility of the court in outing forward spurious causes of action.

We often see that the hard legal analysis comes too late when the lawyers are in advanced settlement negotiations or are in court.

Defendants

4.26 Sometimes a defendant will contest causes of action when there is no basis for doing so.

Where defendants are 'bang to rights' on aspects of the claimant's case they should concede them early or they may risk incurring unnecessary costs. For example, if the defendant in a GDPR and MOPI claim is clearly in breach of the GDPR, then they should consider conceding the GDPR limb at an early stage to keep the costs bills down.

24 *Ibid*, para 24.
25 *Ibid*, para 24.
26 *Stadler v Currys Group Ltd* [2022] EWHC 160 (QB).
27 *Ibid*, paras 78 and 79.

RISK 3 – EXAGGERATED CLAIMS

4.27 If claimants exaggerate their claims they can be penalised on costs.

What is the Rule?

4.28 CPR 44.2(4)(a) says the court will consider the conduct of the parties when making a costs order.

CPR 44.2(5) says that in assessing the conduct of the parties, the court can consider whether the claimant exaggerated its claim.

Why are Exaggerated Claims a Costs Risk in GDPR Claims?

4.29 In data protection claims some claimants have exaggerated their claims when trying to claim for more trivial breaches.

What does the Case Law Say about this?

4.30 Courts take a dim view of exaggerated claims especially when it comes to awarding costs. See, for example, Rolfe *& Others v Veale Wasbrough Vizards LLP*.[28]

Facts:

- The claimant was a mother of a child attending a school. The defendant was the school.
- In 2019, an employee of the defendant accidentally emailed a document which included the claimant's name and information about school fees which were due for payment.
- The recipient of the email responded promptly indicating they thought that the email was not intended for them. The employee replied promptly asking the incorrect recipient to delete the message. The recipient confirmed she had done so.
- The claimant claimed for damages for MOPI, breach of confidence and negligence, together with damages for breach of the GDPR and the DPA 2018, plus a declaration and injunction.[29]

Outcome:

- The case was before the Master in the High Court.

28 *Rolfe & Others v Veale Wasbrough Vizards LLP* [2021] EWHC 2809 (QB) – see https://www.bailii.org/ew/cases/EWHC/QB/2021/2809.html.

29 *Ibid*, paras 1 and 2.

- The Master said:
  - 'We have a plainly exaggerated claim for time spent by the Claimants dealing with the case and a frankly inherently implausible suggestion that the minimal breach caused significant distress and worry or even made them "feel ill".
  - In my judgment no person of ordinary fortitude would reasonably suffer the distress claimed arising in these circumstances in the 21st Century, in a case where a single breach was quickly remedied.
  - I therefore grant summary judgment for the Defendants and dismiss the case with costs [for the Defendants].'[30]

How to Mitigate Against this Risk?

4.31

- The facts need to support claim.
- Clamant lawyers need to advise the claimants of the risks of exaggerating claims not just on costs.
- Claimant lawyers need to be aware of their professional duties on claims. Of course, lawyers must fight for their client's interests but they must do so in a professional way.

RISK 4 – GROUP CLAIMS?

4.32 Costs can be huge in group claims. As a reminder, there are three different types of group claims which can be initiated in the UK:

Type of class action	*In a nutshell*
Group litigation order (GLO) – CPR 19.22	Court makes order for management of multiple claims – appoints lead solicitor, court, cut-off dates for joining
Representative action – CPR 19.8	One or more claimants sue on behalf of larger group
Multiple claims on one claim form – CPR 19.1 and 7.8	Putting multiple claimants on one claim form

See **Chapter 5** for more details on group claims.

30 *Ibid*, paras 12–14.

Why do Group Actions in Data Protection Claims Carry a Costs Risk?

4.33 Group actions are not new in GDPR claims. For example, there were 4 million claimants in *Lloyd v Google*.[31]

The success of group claims has been very mixed.

The costs can be huge. In *Lloyd v Google*, it was reported that the claimant had secured funding for the case of up to £15.5 million (and this was before it even went to the Supreme Court).[32]

What does the Case Law Say?

4.34

- *Weaver and Others v British Airways Plc*[33] – £443,000 of advertising costs incurred by the claimant lawyers who were seeking to publicise the group litigation.[34]
- *Lloyd v Google LLC* – The Supreme Court said 'Persons represented by a representative claimant or defendant will not normally themselves have been joined as parties to the claim, they will not ordinarily be liable to pay any costs incurred by the representative in pursuing (or defending) the claim. That does not prevent the court, if it is in the interests of justice to do so, from making an order requiring a represented person to pay or contribute to costs.'[35]

How to Mitigate Against this Risk?

4.35

- Consider the potential costs of issuing or defending a group action. The appropriate strategy for costs in group actions is as much a commercial matter as a legal matter.
- Be aware of the risks in group litigation costs to date.
- All comes back to getting a clear-eyed view of the merits of claim at the start.

31 *Lloyd v Google* [2021] UK SC 50.
32 Richard Morgan and Ruth Boardman, *Data Protection Strategy*, Sweet & Maxwell, 3rd edn, p 76.
33 *Weaver and Others v British Airways Plc* [2021] EWHC 217 (QB).
34 *Ibid*, paras 1 and 2.
35 *Lloyd v Google LLC* [2021] UKSC 50, para 79.

- Almost like building a house, claimant lawyers must be sure their group action is built on a solid foundation; otherwise, they may go down for some serious costs.
- Many of the larger group actions have struggled in recent years, including *Lloyd v Google, Prismall v Google and VM Morrisons and others.*[36] *Weaver v BA* was more successful for the claimants but did not proceed to a full hearing.

RISK 5 – REFUSING SETTLEMENTS

What does this Mean in GDPR Cases?

4.36 Data protection litigation can be very unpredictable. The issues that you think are key when preparing a claim may not be the key issues at hearing. Cases can take many twists and turns. It is important to be objective when considering whether to settle the case early particularly when a claimant or defendant could be liable for a larger costs bill after the case is head.

A Part 36 offer is a 'without prejudice save as to costs' written offer which is made early in proceedings. It means that if the party doesn't beat the offer at hearing, there will be consequences for them on costs.

Claimants need to be careful about turning down reasonable offers to settle in data protection cases and they should be realistic about what their cases are worth. For example, in *Rolfe and others*, the claimant turned down a Part 36 Offer and subsequently lost her case which had been issued in the High Court. Not only did her data breach case fail but she had to pay many thousands of pounds in costs as well as suffer the embarrassment of being criticised in a reported judgment.

Similarly, if a defendant receives an offer from a claimant, they should consider it carefully. Some larger multi-nationals tend to contest data cases tooth and nail. Defendants need to be realistic about the chances of successfully defending cases.

THE POSITION IN NORTHERN IRELAND AND SCOTLAND

Northern Ireland

4.37 The general rule is that a successful party should recover its costs in Northern Ireland. However, the court has a discretion on costs and can consider

36 *Prismall v Google and VM Morrisons and others* [2024] EWCA Civ 1516 – see https://www.judiciary.uk/wp-content/uploads/2024/12/Prismall-v-Google-UK-Ltd-Approved-judgment-11.12.24.pdf.

the conduct of the parties as well as whether a lodgement was made in court in deciding how to exercise its discretion on costs.[37]

Scotland

4.38 Again, the main rule is that the winning party is awarded expenses against the losing party. The court has a wide discretion, and unreasonable conduct can defeat recovery. Many of the arguments used above under the CPR rules in England and Wales may be relevant in Northern Ireland and Scotland. For example, if a claimant incurs disproportionate costs or behaves unreasonably in a GDPR claim then they may not be awarded their costs even if they win.[38]

TAKEAWAYS

4.39

- **Proportionality** – Parties should not let costs spiral on low-value claims.
- **Unreasonable conduct** – Claimants should avoid 'throwing the kitchen sink' at data claims. More is not always better when it comes to pleading causes of action. Claimants can be penalised on costs for pleading multiple causes of action with no basis in fact or law.

  Equally, defendants should concede matters they have no prospect of defending. For example, if the claimant's information is sent by the defendant to the wrong person in an email, then it usually makes sense to concede that a breach of the GDPR has occurred. You can certainly contest that the defendant suffered damage, but it may make sense to concede on liability so that you can reduce costs.
- **Exaggerated claims** – Courts take a dim view of exaggerated claims.
- **Track allocation** – Courts have been increasingly critical of low value claims being taken in the High Court.
- **Group claims** – Costs in group data protection claims can be many millions of pounds. Lawyers should obtain specialist legal advice on the merits (or de-merits) of group litigation.
- **Refusing to settle** – Where a claimant is strong on the merits in terms of liability, they may consider making a Part 36 offer to settle early. This can be used to their advantage at a later stage when deciding on costs.
- **Cyber insurance** – Companies should make sure they have cyber insurance in place which covers the risk of legal costs.

37 'Litigation and enforcement in Northern Ireland: Overview – Costs', Practical Law, Thomson Reuters.

38 'Expenses: Scotland – Overview', Practical Law, Thomson Reuters.

CHAPTER 5

Group Litigation

INTRODUCTION

5.01 This chapter discusses the different types of group litigation, as well as the relevant case law.

PART I
WHAT IS GROUP LITIGATION?

5.02 Class actions often conjure up images of Hollywood films. You may have seen the movies *A Civil Action* with John Travolta or *Erin Brockovich* with Julia Roberts. In both films, the lawyers took class actions on behalf of wronged plaintiffs against sinister corporations.

In the UK, the more accurate term is 'group litigation' rather than 'class actions'. Group litigation is litigation with two or more claimants. In practice, when dealing with group litigation orders or representative actions, we are usually talking about large numbers of claims.

The purpose of the rules in group litigation or representative actions are to let people with the same or very similar legal problems deal with them together instead of running multiple similar or identical actions separately.

In the UK, group litigation can be hard to get off the ground. It often arises in large scale data breach actions where there can be hundreds of thousands of claimants. Some reports said that the British Airways claim that came from the 2018 data incident had up over 23,000 claimants.[1]

The term 'class action' is not used officially in the UK. The official terms are 'group claims' or 'group litigation'.

There are three different types of group action:

(1) group litigation orders;

(2) representative actions; and

(3) multiple claims on one claim form.

1 Mr Justice Saini at GLO case management hearing.

We consider each of these types of litigation in the first part of this chapter.

Overview

5.03 The summary table below gives an overview of these actions:

Types of group litigation						
Type of class action	**In a nutshell**	**Test**	**Advantages**	**Dis-advantages**	**Costs**	**In practice**
Group litigation order (GLO) – CPR 19.22	Court makes order for manage-ment of multiple claims – appoints lead solicitor, court, cut-off dates for joining	Three-stage: • common or related issues of law or fact; • sufficient no. claims; and • court's discretion.	Either party can ask court to make GLO Court helps manage large and complex actions	Requires claimants to 'opt in'	GLOs have procedure for loser sharing individual and group costs (CPR 46)	GLOs made in British Airways and VM Morrisons data breach cases
Representative action – CPR 19.8	One or more claimants sue on behalf of larger group	Where more than one person has the 'same interest' in a claim	Don't need consent of other parties to sue on their behalf	These are opt out Doesn't work if there are differences in fact or law Damages for each person needs to be assessed individually	Repre-sented persons are not normally liable for costs as they are not parties to the claim	Repre-sentative data cases have struggled, eg, *Prismall v Google* and *Lloyd v Google* were both unsuc-cessful
Multiple claims on one claim form – CPR 19.1 and 7.8	Putting multiple claimants on one claim form	Can it be 'con-veniently disposed of in same proceedings'	Less stringent test than GLO	Better suited to smaller actions	Reduces costs	*Angel v Black Horse* case sets out criteria

What is the Difference Between Opt In and Opt Out?

5.04 **Opt out**: Representative actions are 'opt out'; which means that claimants are automatically included. For example, in *Lloyd v Google* 4 million iPhone users were automatically included in the claim. The claimants were alleging that Google tracked some of the behaviour of iPhone users in the UK. All iPhone users were automatically included in the claim. Claimants can receive compensation for a case they never knew existed. A claimant can opt out of the claim if they wish.

Opt in: In group litigation orders, claimants must opt in if they want to receive compensation. For example, after the 2018 British Airways data breach, claimants had to opt in if they wanted to be a part of the action. Claimant solicitors had to advertise to get the claimants to join the claim.

Group Litigation in the UK – Myth Busting

5.05

- **Myth 1 – Class actions are 'not allowed' in the UK**. This is not accurate. There are three mechanisms for group litigation in the UK, group litigation orders, representative actions and multiple claims on one claim form. The thresholds in the UK for getting one of these forms of group litigation off the ground are more stringent than those for US class actions.
- **Myth 2 – No group litigation claims have yet succeeded**. This is not accurate. Numerous group litigation claims involving data protection have failed (eg, *Prismall v Google* and *Lloyd v Google*). However, other group claims have been more successful. For example, in the British Airways group litigation (which did not proceed to a full hearing) thousands of claimants received compensation when the case settled. We consider each of these cases in detail later in this chapter.
- **Myth 3 – If the ICO fine a company for a large data breach this means that all the affected persons will automatically get compensation**. This is incorrect. Claimants must prove loss and damage relating to the data breach if they are to obtain compensation in court. The mere fact that their data was caught up in a data breach does not necessarily mean they will receive compensation in the courts.

What Types of Group Litigation do we See in Data Protection Claims?

5.06 Group claims are an important part of data protection litigation. This is because data protection laws and GDPR infringements can affect large numbers of claimants.

Examples of types of group claims in data protection:

- **Data breach claims taken by customers** – where a defendant has lost the data of many data subjects such as the British Airways claims (see below).
- **Data breach claims taken by employees** – where a defendant has lost the data of many employees, such as the VM Morrison case (see below).

- **Breaches data protection rights** – where large numbers of people claim for breach of their data protection rights. For example, *Lloyd v Google* case where it was alleged that Google secretly tracked the internet activity of millions of Apple iPhone users in breach of the fair and lawfulness principle in the Data Protection Act (DPA 1998).
- **Misuse of private information claims** – where large numbers of people claim for breach of a privacy related cause of action such as misuse of private information. In *Prismall v Google UK* (see below) the claimant brought a representative action on behalf of approximately 1.6 million NHS patients against Google for alleged misuse of private information.

Why are Group Claims Becoming More Prominent?

5.07 There are numerous reasons why mass claims in data protection are becoming more prominent.

- **GDPR means people are informed when their data has been compromised**

  Individuals are more likely to hear about breaches affecting their data than they were in the past. As the Information Commissioner's Office (ICO) says:

  > The UK GDPR introduces a duty on all organisations to report certain personal data breaches … (to) individuals without undue delay.

- **Breaches are more widely reported**[2]

  Under the GDPR, the ICO can issue maximum UK GDPR fines up to £17.5 million or 4% of total annual worldwide turnover. These fines get a lot of publicity in the mainstream press.

- **Mass data collection means larger scale data breaches and more claims**

  Lord Legatt said at para 67 of *Lloyd v Google*:

  > The development of digital technologies had added to the potential for mass harm for which legal redress may be sought in such cases.

- **More favourable legal climate**

  The legal principles are evolving and the legal principles for claiming for GDPR infringements are, arguably, becoming favourable to claimants.

  In *Farley v Paymaster Ltd*,[3] the Court of Appeal said claims for breach of GDPR do not require a 'threshold of seriousness'. It said:

  > A claim to be compensated for annoyance or irritation caused by fear of third-party misuse is tenable, provided the fear is well-founded.[4]

2 The GDPR makes organisations report some data breaches under Articles 33 and 34.
3 *Farley v Paymaster Ltd* [2025] EWCA Civ 1117.
4 *Ibid*, para 93.

PART 2
GROUP LITIGATION ORDERS IN ENGLAND AND WALES – OVERVIEW

What is a Group Litigation Order?

5.08 A group litigation order or GLO is a court order which allows similar individual claims to be managed together so that similar issues within each claim can be decided together.

Are GLOs Fitting for Large-scale Data Breach Actions?

5.09 GLOs in large data breach actions allow courts to decide common issues together.

For example, if there are 1,000 claimants in a data breach action then the court can decide the common issues for all claimants together such as deciding whether the defendant has breached the GDPR. This saves the claimants, defendants and court system time and resource.

Are GLOs Opt In or Opt Out?

5.10 GLOs follow an opt-in procedure. This means that an individual must actively sign up to join the group litigation.[5]

What is the Test for Making a GLO?

5.11 The court has a power to make a group litigation order for 'the case management of claims which give rise to common or related issues of fact or law' (CPR 19.21).

The test is within the CPR rules. CPR 19.22 says '(1) The court may make a GLO where there are or are likely to be a number of claims giving rise to the GLO issues. The multiple parties may be claimants or defendants.'

This is fully at the court's discretion.

5 Jeremy Sher, partner, and Leontia McArdle, Legal Director, DLA Piper, 'Group litigation and group litigation orders', Practical Law, Thomson Reuters – this article is particularly useful on the subject of GLO costs.

In *Abernethy and Others v Barclays Bank UK Plc and others*[6] the court said the test for granting a GLO was:

(1) Do the claims have 'common or related issues of law or fact'?

(2) Are there or are likely to be a number of claims giving rise to those common or related issues of law or fact?

(3) If the tests at (1) and (2) are met, this gives rise to a consideration as to whether to exercise the court's discretionary power to make a GLO.

The Procedural Rules for Making a GLO

5.12 The next section is heavy on the procedure around GLOs. If you have no interest in the procedural rules on GLOs you may wish to skip to the next section on representative actions.

The procedure for making a GLO is set out at Practice Direction 19B.[7] The procedure for GLOs is set out in CPR 19.21–19.26.

Preliminary Steps

5.13 In Practice Direction 19.B on GLOs, it says that certain preliminary steps should be taken including:

- the solicitor acting for the proposed applicant should consult the Law Society's Multi Party Action Information Service to obtain information about GLOs; and
- the solicitors may want to form a 'Solicitors Group' and appoint a lead solicitor.

Making the Application for the GLO

5.14 When making the application for the GLO (which can be made by the claimant or the defendant), the applicant should include details about:

- the *nature* of the litigation;
- the *claims* already issued;
- the *number* of parties;
- the *common issues of fact or law*;

6 *Abernethy and Others v. Barclays Bank UK Plc and others* [2025] EWCC 1 – see https://3vb.com/wp-content/uploads/2025/09/Abernethy.pdf. See para 27 of judgment.

7 See the Gov website at: https://www.justice.gov.uk/courts/procedure-rules/civil/rules/part19/pd_part19b.

- whether *any smaller groups of claims within the group are different* in any way from the wider group.

Consult Practice Direction 19.B 3.2 if you want to know precise details about the procedure.

Whilst it is usually a claimant or defendant who will make an application for a GLO, the court can make a GLO order of its own volition.[8]

If the GLO is Made, What Kinds of Things will it Refer to?

5.15 Specify the GLO issues which will identify the claims to be managed as a group under the GLO.[9]

GLO Register

5.16 Once the GLO is made a group register is set up to keep track of all the various issues relation to the GLO.[10]

Cut-off Dates

5.17 Claimant solicitors will need to make sure they get all the claimants on board before the deadline.

The management court may specify a date after which no claim may be added to the Group Register unless the court gives permission.[11]

Pleadings

5.18 The court may direct that the GLO claimants serve group particulars of claim rather than multiple different particulars of claims.

8 Practice Direction 19B.4.
9 CPR 19.22.
10 Under 19.22:
'(2) A GLO must –
(a) contain directions about the establishment of a register (the 'group register') on which the claims managed under the GLO will be entered;'
Also, consult CPR 6.1–6.6 if you want to know the precise details of the procedure relating to the register.
11 Practice Direction 19B.13.

Getting specialist legal advice on how to draft the pleadings in group litigation would be advisable.[12]

In *Spurgeon & Ors v Capita Plc*,[13] the High Court dismissed an application for strike out on behalf of the defendants. This case arose out of an alleged data breach at Capita. A total of 3,973 claimants sued the defendants for compensation for breach under the GDPR and the DPA 2018. The defendants alleged that the pleadings in the case were exaggerated. The defendants said 'the claimants' solicitors have improperly advanced certain assertions within the Particulars of Claim regarding the mental consequences allegedly sustained by the claimants, and have so acted as to taint their clients' beliefs and evidence as to them that the entirety of the claims have become an abuse of process, and that this is so serious as to require the court to strike out the entirety of all of the claims'.[14]

The defendants' application to strike out was unsuccessful.[15]

The court further said in rejecting the defendants' application that that 'pleadings are not witness statements or evidence. They are simply a statement of the asserted facts upon which a claimant relies to assert a claim in law (and CPR16.4 provides that the POC must comprise a concise statement of such facts). In due course in the litigation (assuming it proceeds), each claimant will provide a witness statement(s) (from themselves and/or others) which will set out their own factual history and evidence as to their mental etc. states in detail. Those witness statements (unlike the pleadings) are to be the witness's own words, and, if a lawyer may have drafted them on instructions, are to contain those words. They (and not the pleadings) are the evidence at trial, and where they can be tested by cross-examination. The stage of witness statements has not yet been reached.'[16]

Costs and GLOs

5.19 If the group litigation is unsuccessful then each claimant will usually be responsible for:

- its own individual costs; and
- the common costs which will be divided between all the claimants.

CPR 46.6 sets out the position for costs on GLOs.

12 Practice Direction 19B.14.
13 *Spurgeon & Ors v Capita Plc* [2026] EWHC 241 (KB).
14 *Ibid*, paras 1–2.
15 *Ibid*, para 233.
16 *Ibid*, para 166.

In the case of *Greenwood v Goodwin*[17] the court said that it had a wide latitude in deciding costs in GLOs.

See **Chapter 4** for more details on costs.[18]

Are GLOs only Made in the High Court?

5.20 GLO orders can be made in the High Court or the county court[19].

PART 3
REPRESENTATIVE ACTIONS

5.21 A representative action is another way of taking a group action.

Representative proceedings are set out in CPR 19.8.

Under CPR 19.8 a claimant can bring a claim as a 'representative' of all the other claimants if they all have the 'same interest' in the claim.

The court has discretion in deciding whether to allow a representative claim to proceeds.

Is the Outcome of Representative Actions Binding?

5.22 CPR 19.8(4) sets out that the judgment or order of the court is binding on all the parties unless the court orders otherwise.

What does 'Same Interest' Mean?

5.23 The parties must be able to show that the represented parties have the 'same interest' in the litigation 'for all practical purposes' before the court will exercise its discretion to allow the representative action to succeed.

The Supreme Court in *Lloyd v Google LLC* set out the following points on the same interest test:

(1) **Discretion**: Where the same interest requirement is satisfied, the court has a discretion whether to allow a claim to proceed as a representative action.

17 *Greenwood v Goodwin* [2014] EWHC 227 (Ch), paras 25–28. – see https://www.bailii.org/cgi-bin/format.cgi?doc=/ew/cases/EWHC/Ch/2014/227.html&query=(greenwood)+AND+(v)+AND+(goodwin).

18 See also Practice Direction 19.B, para 16.

19 Practice Direction 19B.3.5–3.7 in the Chancery Division with the consent of the Chancellor of the High Court; or in the county court with the consent of the Head of Civil Justice.

(2) **No Requirement of consent**: As the ability to act as a representative under the rule does not depend on the consent of the persons represented, the represented class doesn't need to be aware of the existence of the action.

(3) **Class of persons**: It is desirable that the class of persons represented should be clearly defined.

(4) **Costs**: Persons represented by a representative claimant or defendant will not ordinarily be liable to pay any costs.[20]

(5) **Damages**: Representative actions are *not* a suitable vehicle if an individualised assessment for damages is required.[21] For example, if there are 100 claimants in a data breach in which medical data were lost but each suffered a different level of anxiety as a result of their medical data being lost, then a representative action is not the appropriate way to take the claim.

The court said that there could be a bifurcated (ie, two-branch) case where the representative action could be used to decide on common issues of law. For example, the representative action could consider whether the defendant did in fact breach the GDPR.

However, the court said that the representative action could not be used to decide individual issues such as quantum. For example, if each claimant has suffered different loss.

PART 4
JOINING MULTIPLE DEFENDANTS IN THE SAME CLAIM FORM

5.24 The first mechanism to consider for group litigation is joining multiple claimants (or defendants) in the same claim form.

CPR 19.1 states that 'Any number of claimants or defendants may be joined as parties to a claim.'

CPR 7.3 states that:

> A claimant may use a single claim form to start all claims which can be conveniently disposed of in the same proceedings.

Having multiple claims on the same claim form is known as 'an omnibus claim'. The advantages to taking an omnibus claim is that it might be simpler than engaging in the complexities of a GLO or representative action. For example, if seven employees suffer a data breach at work, then their solicitor might put all the claims on one claim form.

20 *Lloyd v Google LLC* [2021] UKSC 50, paras 75–79.
21 *Ibid*, para 80.

Case Law on Joining Multiple Defendants to the Same Claim form

5.25 The case *Angel v Black Horse Ltd* sets out the legal position on this type of group litigation.[22]

Relevant factors include:

- the number of claimants;
- whether there are multiple claimants suing the same defendant or multiple defendants;
- whether the claims relate to the same matters or different matters;
- whether the claims involve the same causes of action;
- whether the issues are likely to be common issues;
- whether the case-specific claims and defences do or are likely to raise common issues of law or fact;
- whether decisions in lead or test cases will be significant for the disposal of following cases;
- whether the overriding objective is better met by separate claim forms or an omnibus claim form; and
- whether all or some of the claims will more conveniently be disposed of together.

WHAT IS THE POSITION IN SCOTLAND AND NORTHERN IRELAND?

5.26 The processes above relate to group actions in England and Wales.

In relation to Northern Ireland, refer to Order 15 of the Court Rules.[23]

In relation to Scotland, refer to Part 4 of the Civil Litigation (Expenses and Group Proceedings) (Scotland) Act 2018.[24]

22 *Angel v Black Horse Ltd* [2025] EWHC 490 (KB) – see https://caselaw.nationalarchives.gov.uk/ewhc/kb/2025/490.

23 Fox, O'Shiel, Diver, Flanagan Marlowe, 'Litigation and Enforcement in NI', Practical Law, Thomson Reuters.

24 'Group Proceedings Scotland: Overview', Practical Law, Thomson Reuters.

PART 5
GROUP LITIGATION ORDER CASE LAW

Case: *WM Morrison Supermarkets plc vs Various Claimants* [2020] UKSC 12[25]

5.27 **Court**: Supreme Court

Date: 1 April 2020

Type of group litigation: GLO[26]

Number of claimants: 9,263 employees or former employees of Morrisons[27]

Cause of action: Breach of section 4(4) of the DPA 2018, misuse of private information, and breach of confidence.[28]

Result: Claimants' claim unsuccessful. The defendant was not liable for the actions of a rogue employee.

Factual background (paras 2–8):

- In November 2013, an employee of Morrisons downloaded payroll data he was entrusted with at work onto a personal USB stick and took it home.
- In January 2014, to satisfy a grudge, he uploaded the data of 100,000 Morrisons employees onto a file-sharing website and also sent it to newspapers.
- He was arrested, convicted of several offences and sentenced to eight years' imprisonment.
- Over 5,500 employees, whose personal data had been disclosed, issued a claim against Morrisons claiming damages for breach of the DPA 2018 and/ or for the misuse of private information and/or breach of confidence.
- The High Court made a GLO in respect of the claims
- Morrisons had spent more than £2.26m in dealing with the immediate aftermath of the disclosure.
- The court found that that Morrisons was not vicariously liable for the actions of the employee when he deliberately disclosed the data of 100,000 employees.[29]

25 https://www.supremecourt.uk/cases/uksc-2018-0213.
26 *WM Morrison Supermarkets plc vs Various Claimants*, para 10.
27 *Ibid*, para 2.
28 *Ibid*, para 9.
29 *Ibid*, para 2.

What the court said about GLOs: The High Court made a GLO in connection with the claims. Ten lead claimants were selected, with the remainder of the claims being stayed pending judgment.[30]

Case: *Weaver and Others v British Airways Plc* [2021] EWHC 217 (QB)

5.28 **Court**: High Court, Queen's Bench Division

Date: 2 February 2021

Type of group litigation: GLO

Number of claimants: 22,230[31]

Cause of action: Official record doesn't say although likely a breach of the GDPR claim as court said 'litigation concerns claims for damages … (relating to) a cyber-attack on BA's systems … containing customer personal data'.

Result: GLO granted. Case did not run to full hearing and was settled with no admission of liability.

Factual background:

- The litigation followed a cyber-attack on British Airways' (BA) electronic systems. The attack compromised systems containing personal data on BA's website and mobile application.
- GLO was made by the High Court in 2019.
- The claimant applied to extend the cut-off date.
- An issue of costs arose (ie, about which costs were recoverable).[32]

What the court said about GLOs:

The court extended the cut-off date to join the litigation by two months to allow the most recent claimant law firm advertising to bear fruit.

After that no further claimants would be allowed to join the action.

The court also disallowed advertising costs incurred by the claimants' solicitors advertising for claimants.

They were general overheads and were therefore not recoverable.[33]

30 *Ibid*, para 10.

31 *Weaver and Others v British Airways Plc*, para 21 – see https://www.bailii.org/ew/cases/EWHC/QB/2021/217.html.

32 *Ibid*, paras 1 and 2.

33 See also 'British Airways settles data breach class action', Practical Law, Thomson Reuters.

PART 6
REPRESENTATIVE ACTION CASES

Case: *Lloyd v Google LLC* [2021] UKSC 50

5.29 **Court**: Supreme Court.[34]

Date: 10 November 2021

Type of group litigation: Representative action[35]

Number of claimants: Estimated at 4 million. The claim for each claimant was £750. This would produce damages of £3 billion.[36]

Cause of action: Breach of section 4(4) of the Data Protection Act 1998 (DPA 1998).[37]

Result: Claim unsuccessful. Breach of the DPA 1998 needed proof of actual damage not mere loss of control of information.[38]

Factual background:

The claim alleged that, for several months in late 2011 and early 2012, Google secretly tracked the internet activity of millions of Apple iPhone users and used the data collected in this way for commercial purposes without the users' knowledge or consent and alleged breach of the fair and lawfulness principle under the DPA 1998.[39] This was through the alleged use of the 'Safari workaround' to bypass privacy settings on Apple iPhones.[40]

What the court said about GLOs:

A representative action is not suitable where an individualised assessment of damages for each claimant is necessary. However, a representative action may be appropriate where the court is deciding on issue of liability or legal principles. [41]

The key passage in *Lloyd v Google*:

> What limits the scope for claiming damages in representative proceedings is the compensatory principle on which damages for a civil wrong are awarded with the object of putting the claimant – as an individual – in the same position, as best money can do it, as if the wrong had not occurred. In the

34 https://caselaw.nationalarchives.gov.uk/ewhc/kb/2025/490.
35 *Lloyd v Google LLC*, para 5.
36 *Ibid.*
37 *Ibid*, para 1.
38 *Ibid*, para 159.
39 *Ibid*, para 1 and 18.
40 *Ibid*, para 9.
41 *Ibid*, paras 80 and 81.

> ordinary course, this necessitates an individualised assessment which raises no common issue and cannot fairly or effectively be carried out without the participation in the proceedings of the individuals concerned. A representative action is therefore not a suitable vehicle for such an exercise.[42]

Costs in representative actions:

With respect to costs, the court said:

> Persons represented by a representative claimant or defendant will not normally themselves have been joined as parties to the claim, they will not ordinarily be liable to pay any costs incurred by the representative in pursuing (or defending) the claim. That does not prevent the court, if it is in the interests of justice to do so, from making an order requiring a represented person to pay or contribute to costs.[43]

The lowest common denominator argument didn't work because the claimant was saying that there was a base level of harm that affected all claimants. The court's view was that this didn't work when the base level of harm didn't reach the threshold required for damages.[44]

Case: *Prismall v Google UK Limited and another* [2024] EWCA Civ 1516[45]

5.30 **Court**: Court of Appeal

Date: 11 December 2024

Type of group litigation: Representative action

Number of claimants: 1.6 million[46]

Cause of action: The tort of misuse of private information (MOPI)

Result: Claim struck out. The Court of Appeal said that the claimants did not have a reasonable prospect of establishing MOPI. The court said that bringing a representative action on these facts was difficult owing to each claimant's reasonable expectation of privacy differing across a large group.[47]

The court said 'There will normally be an expectation of privacy for any patient unidentifiable information … However the tort involved a threshold

42 *Ibid*, paras 80 and 81.
43 *Ibid*, para 79.
44 *Ibid*, paras 145–147.
45 This case is one of the key cases on representative actions relating to personal information.
46 *Prismall v Google UK Limited and another*, para 1.
47 *Ibid*, paras 63, 65, 66.

of seriousness. A claim for Misuse of Private Information will not invariably succeed where a patient has placed medical information in the public domain.'[48]

Factual background:

- Mr Prismall brought a representative action for the tort of misuse of private information against Google UK and DeepMind.
- The action was on behalf of Mr Prismall and a class of person said to number approximately 1.6 million.
- The claim was for damages of a one-off transfer by the Royal NHS Free Trust of data between 2015 and 2017 to Google and DeepMind, who used that data to develop an app called Streams which was intended to be used to identify patients suffering from kidney injury.[49]
- Mr Prismall had extensive treatment at the Royal Free Hospital.
- He did not consent to his private medical information being collected, transferred, stored or used by Google and DeepMind.[50]
- In October 2015, Google and DeepMind applied to the NHS Research Ethics Committee for approval for a project entitled 'using machine learning to improve prediction of acute kidney injury and general patient deterioration'.[51]
- The High Court struck out the action because the representative class could not establish a reasonable expectation of privacy[52] and that the 'same interest' test was not satisfied.
- The Court of Appeal upheld the High Court's decision – it said that even though medical information is generally private, the tort requires a threshold of seriousness and everything will depend on the circumstances.[53]
- Because there were different levels of damages for the claimants (some may have placed medical information in the public domain), liability itself could not be determined on a 'class-wide' basis.
- The court rejected a common denominator argument (ie, that all claimants suffered some minimal harm). [54]

What the court said about GLOs:

> We consider that a representative class claim for Misuse of Private Information is always going to be very difficult to bring. This is because relevant circumstances will affect whether there is a reasonable expectation

48 *Ibid*, paras 62, 65.
49 *Ibid*, para 2.
50 *Ibid*, para 11.
51 *Ibid*, para 15.
52 *Ibid*, paras 4 and 7.
53 *Ibid*, para 63.
54 'Strike out of representative claim for privacy damages upheld (Court of Appeal)', 13 December 2024, Practical Law, Thomson Reuters.

of privacy for any particular claimant, which will itself affect whether all of the represented class have 'the same interest'.[55]

PART 7
CONCLUSION

Litigation Strategy

5.31 It can be a challenge in the UK trying to get group actions off the ground. Claimants must consider whether it makes sense to start group litigation in a data protection claim. They should consider:

- costs issues;
- the strength of the evidence;
- the merits or de merits of the claim;
- the complexities of the CPR rules and the court system;
- the likelihood of an early settlement; and
- whether there has been a regulator finding for the GDPR infringement against the defendants.

TAKEAWAYS

5.32

(1) **Which type of litigation**. Claimants need an understanding of:

- the strengths and weaknesses of their case; and
- the processes for each type of group action.

Consider getting specialist legal advice on the merits of the claim.

(2) **Results have been very mixed for large-scale data protection and privacy actions to date**. For example, *Lloyd v Google* and *Prismall v Google* failed although both were brought under the pre-GDPR regime. On the other hand, some large group actions have settled with no admission of liability (eg, the British Airways cases relating to the 2018 cyber incident).

(3) **Legally the picture is also mixed**. *Farley v Paymaster* has lowered the bar for claiming damages for breach of the GDPR and the DPA 2018 as there is no threshold for seriousness for such claims.

(4) **Being on the wrong side of group litigation is still a risk for companies**. Companies should put compliance measures in place to protect against large-scale data breaches. British Airways' website was hacked, and this

55 *Prismall v Google UK Limited and another*, para 66.

caused a world of difficulties for it in terms of the ICO fine, group litigation and reputational damage.

(5) **Prevention is always better than cure when it comes to data protection.** Parties need to put strong systems and controls in place on data protection to reduce the likelihood of events which give risk to litigation. For example, they may wish to consider the following steps:

- **Risk Register**: The risk department and chief risk officer in any large companies should know about the risk that data breaches pose to their business including regulator fines and group actions. The cost of group actions can dwarf regulator fines. For example, some reports suggest that the British Airways settlement cost £80 million, several times the amount it was fined by the regulator (ie, £20 million).
- **Policies**: Companies should have company policies in place to ensure data protection standards are enforced throughout the organisation. They should have robust data breach response procedures so that the company can spring into action if the worst-case scenario ever happens to limit the damage.
- **Encryption**: The author suggests that proper encryption standards and policies can cover a multitude of risks when it comes to data security. If companies get their encryption posture right, then they can avoid much of the pain that comes because encryption can render data useless to hackers if it ever does fall into their hands. With the rise of quantum computing, proper encryption standards are becoming harder to meet so it is more important than ever to invest in state-of-the-art encryption.
- **Training**: Most data breaches are caused by staff making mistakes such as clicking on malicious links sent by hackers. Train staff so they can avoid data breaches.

(6) **Costs**: Samuel Butler famously said 'In law, nothing is certain but the expense.' Consider the potential costs of issuing or defending a group action. The appropriate strategy for costs in group actions is as much a commercial matter as a legal matter. See **Chapter 4** for more details on costs.

CHAPTER 6

Suing for Breach of the GDPR Principles

INTRODUCTION

6.01 The GDPR sets out seven main principles:

(1) lawfulness, fairness and transparency;

(2) purpose limitation;

(3) data minimisation;

(4) accuracy;

(5) storage limitation;

(6) security; and

(7) accountability (this principle is about controllers keeping records and will rarely, if ever, lead to litigation).

The purpose of these principles is to say very clearly that personal data belongs to the individuals to whom it relates; it is not owned by corporations to do with it as they please.

In this chapter we consider how claimants can sue for compensation because of the defendant breaching the GDPR data protection principles.

Personal data must be processed in a way which is consistent with these principles. If it is processed in a way that is:

- inconsistent with these principles; and
- causes loss or damage to a person,

then that person can sue for compensation under the GDPR.

The first (fairness and lawfulness) and sixth (security) principles are the principles which give rise to the most data protection claims. The first principle is discussed in detail below.

The sixth principle (security) is very important and is discussed in **Chapter 7**.

Often a claimant will claim that the defendant has breached several of the principles. For example, in the case of *Vidal-Hall v Google*,[1] the claimant alleged that the defendant breached the first, second, fifth and sixth data protection principles.

We also look at the rules on marketing and how data protection litigation may arise there.

PART I
AN OVERVIEW OF THE DATA PROTECTION PRINCIPLES

6.02

Executive summary of this chapter	
GDPR principle which may give rise to a claim	**In practice**
Fairness, lawfulness and transparency principle	Claimant alleges that processing was unfair or unlawful or not transparent A very wide ground which has been a fertile ground for data protection. litigation. See *Campbell v MGN* [2004] UKHL 22, *Law Society v Kordowski* [2014] EWHC 3057 (QB)
Purpose limitation	Claimant alleges that data were collected for one purpose and used for another, eg, in the Cambridge Analytica scandal, the ICO found that data collected by Facebook was used by political parties to target people with political ads.[2]
Data limitation principle	Claimant alleges excessive data processing, eg, the privacy activist Max Schrems complained that Facebook processed excessive data about him[3]
Accuracy	Claimant sues for damage related to the processing of inaccurate data about them In *Aven & Ors v Orbis Business Intelligence Ltd* [2020] EWHC 1812 (QB), the claimants were awarded £18k when the defendants processed data about them which was inaccurate
Storage limitation	Claimant alleges that old or obsolete data about them was not deleted.
Security	Claimant sues for data being lost or compromised – see **Chapter 7**

1 *Vidal-Hall v Google* [2015] EWCA 311.
2 https://ico.org.uk/for-the-public/ico-40/cambridge-analytica-raids/.
3 https://www.bbc.co.uk/news/articles/c4gr4r5ln03o.

PRINCIPLE 1 – THE FAIRNESS, LAWFULNESS AND TRANSPARENCY PRINCIPLE

Principle 1

6.03 Along with security, this is the most important principle from a data protection litigation standpoint.

Article 5(1) of the UK GDPR demands that:

> Personal data shall be processed lawfully, fairly and in a transparent manner in relation to the data subject.

A claimant may allege that the data processing was:

- unfair in some way; and/or
- in breach of some law; and/or
- not transparent in some way.

Lawfulness

6.04 When is data processing unlawful?

Data processing must be carried out in accordance with all applicable law.

When data processing is carried out contrary to the law then a claimant may have a claim for compensation if the claimant can prove that the unlawful processing caused damage.

A defendant may process personal data unlawfully in two ways:

(1) processing data without having an appropriate legal basis in place under the GDPR; and/or (see para **6.05** below); or

(2) processing data contrary to specific law, eg, the Human Rights Act 1998 (see para **6.09** below).

Unlawful processing claims – claims where the defendant does not have an appropriate legal basis in place

6.05 When a controller processes personal data relating to a particular individual, it must have a legal basis in place that allows it to carry out that processing. No controller can ever process personal data without having a legal basis in place. For example, a company may seek an individual's consent to process their data. Alternatively, it may rely on 'contractual necessity' to process the person's data.

We often see companies face litigation because they didn't have an appropriate legal basis in place.

The legal bases for processing appear at Article 6 of the GDPR, as set out below:

(a) Consent of the data subject – the data subject has given consent to the processing of his or her personal data.

(b) Contractual necessity – processing is necessary for the performance of a contract.[4]

(c) Legal obligation – processing is necessary for compliance with a legal obligation.[5]

(d) Vital interests of an individual – processing is necessary in order to protect the vital interests of the data subject or of another person.[6]

(e) Performance of a task in the public interest – processing is necessary for the performance of a task carried out in the public interest.[7]

(f) Legitimate interest of your firm – processing is necessary for the purposes of the legitimate interests pursued by the controller or by a third party.[8]

See the GDPR, Article 6 for more details on these legal bases.

Controllers must choose one appropriate legal basis for processing. There is no one legal basis that works better than the other available legal bases, but it is up to the data controller to decide which legal basis is most appropriate in the circumstances based on the type of data processing they are doing and on its relationship with the data subject. Controllers must be careful about choosing their lawful basis; if it is not a valid or legally defensible legal basis, then they may potentially be breaching the GDPR and open themselves up to litigation.

Special category personal data and legal bases

6.06 The litigation risk is higher when the controller is processing special category personal data (such as race, health, sexuality data). If a controller is processing sensitive personal data relating to a data subject, then it needs one of the Article 6 legal basis above. There is also a further legal basis set out in Article 9 of the GDPR (eg, explicit consent, vital interests).

Web scraping cases

6.07 There has been a proliferation of 'web scraping' cases where companies use bots to collect vast quantities of personal data from publicly accessible

4 GDPR, Article 6(1)(b).
5 GDPR, Article 6(1)(c).
6 GDPR, Article 6(1)(d).
7 GDPR, Article 6(1)(e).
8 GDPR, Article 6(1)(f).

websites across the internet. For example, they might collect names and email addresses from social media sites or professional networks such as LinkedIn. Often the web scraping company has no relationship whatsoever with the data subjects. If these web scrapers collect data without having a legal basis in place, then they may open themselves up to litigation.

No legal basis in place – a fertile ground for litigation?

6.08 The legal basis rules are a fertile ground for litigation.

If a defendant in litigation does not have a valid legal basis in place for the processing it performed on the defendant's data, then it will be at risk of having to pay damages.

For example, if the defendant has no legal basis and obtained the claimant's data when they bought it from list sellers, then the claimant will have a potential claim.

Similarly, if the defendant has relied on a legal basis such as consent but it cannot show that the consent is valid, then the claimant will have a potential claim.

Unlawful processing claims – claims where the defendant's processing was contrary to a non-data protection law

6.09 A claimant has a potential claim if they can show that the data processing conducted by the defendant was unlawful (ie, if it was contrary to any law).

Mr Justice Tugendhat said in the case *Law Society v Kordowski* that 'the reference to "lawfully" in the First Data Protection Principle applies to any form of conduct that is unlawful including breach of confidence, libel and harassment'.[9]

The ICO sets out that:

> processing may be unlawful if it results in:
>
> - a breach of a duty of confidence
> - your organisation exceeding its legal powers or exercising those powers improperly
> - an infringement of copyright
> - a breach of an enforceable contractual agreement
> - a breach of industry-specific legislation or regulations; or
> - a breach of the Human Rights Act 1998.
>
> … this list is not exhaustive … processing personal data in breach of copyright or industry regulations (for example) will involve unlawful processing.

9 *Law Society v Kordowski* [2011] EWHC 3185 (QB), para 78 – see https://www.bailii.org/ew/cases/EWHC/QB/2011/3185.html.

In other words, if the data processing is in breach of any other UK law, then it is unlawful data processing and therefore could be in breach of the first principle under the GDPR.

Does the defendant have to breach a UK law for the processing to be unlawful?

6.10 Yes, if the defendant is claiming the processing is unlawful due to the breach of a non-data protection law (eg, the defendant is claiming that the processing was in breach of employment law), then the legal infringement must be part of UK law (or EU law if someone is pursuing a claim in an EU court for breach of the EU GDPR).[10]

Unlawful processing – case law example

6.11 **Case**: *Law Society v Kordowski* [2011] EWHC 3185 (QB)

Court: High Court (Queen's Bench Division), Media & Communications List

Date: 7 December 2011

Type: Group claim

Full judgment: https://uk.practicallaw.thomsonreuters.com/D-012-2813?transitionType=Default&contextData=(sc.Default).

Who and what happened

- The defendant was the publisher of a website called 'Solicitors from Hell'.
- Members of the public were invited to 'name and shame' solicitors.[11]
- The defendant was described by the court as a 'vexatious litigant and a public nuisance'.[12]
- The claimants were the Law Society and group of solicitors.
- The causes of action were libel, harassment under the Protection from Harassment Act 1997 and breach of the Data Protection Act 1998.

Outcome

- The claimants were successful. The defendants were found to have processed personal data 'in a grossly unfair and unlawful way by, in particular (a) publishing highly offensive defamatory allegations about these solicitors and individuals on the website (b) pursuing a course of conduct against

10 Peter Carey (ed) (2020), *Data Protection: A Practical Guide to UK Law*, Oxford University Press, 6th edn, p 68.
11 *Law Society v Kordowski* [2011] EWHC 3185 (QB), para 1.
12 *Ibid*, para 183.

these solicitors and other individuals that amounts to harassment contrary to the Protection from Harassment Act 1997'.[13]

- The claimants were granted a perpetual injunction by the court prohibiting further publication of the solicitors from hell website.[14]

Fairness

6.12 The ICO puts it best when it says:

> Processing of personal data must always be fair as well as lawful. If any aspect of your processing is unfair you will be in breach of this principle – even if you can show that you have a lawful basis for the processing.
>
> In general, fairness means that you should only handle personal data in ways that people would reasonably expect and not use it in ways that have unjustified adverse effects on them.[15]

Was the claimant misled in any way in terms of the collection or the processing of the personal data? Was the processing exploitative or underhand in any way? Was the data processing unexpected?

For example, let's imagine that:

- A company called 'Underhand Marketing' collect data from web scraping.
- Claire's name was collected via web scraping.
- Underhand sell Claire's data to one their clients, a payday loan provider called 'High Interest Loans'.
- High Interest Loans send Claire emails trying to get her to use their services.
- Claire makes a data subject access request for information as she wants to understand how High Interest obtained her data.
- When she learns that they bought if from Underhand who obtained it from web scraping, she believes her data were unfairly processed.
- Claire sues Underhand and High Interest for unfairly processing her data.

The concept of fairness can be quite wide and therefore it can be a useful ground for claimants to lean in cases where defendants have processed their data in way which is unusual or unexpected.

13 *Ibid*, para 89.
14 *Ibid*, para 184.
15 ICO, 'Principle (a): Lawfulness, fairness and transparency', https://ico.org.uk/for-organisations/uk-gdpr-guidance-and-resources/data-protection-principles/a-guide-to-the-data-protection-principles/lawfulness-fairness-and-transparency/.

Case law on fairness

6.13 **Case**: *Anthony Woolley and Deborah Woolley v Nahib Akbar Or Akram* [2017] SC Edin 7[16]

Court: Scottish Sheriff Court

Date: 3 February 2017

Cause of action: Breach of principles under the Data Protection Act 1998:

(1) lawfulness, fairness and transparency principle;

(2) data minimisation principle; and

(3) storage limitation principle.

Facts:

- The pursuers lived above a guest house which was owned by the defenders.
- The defenders installed security cameras and audio recording devices which were highly intrusive.
- They recorded 24 hours per day.

Result:

- Amongst other breaches the court found that the processing of personal data by the defenders was unfair. The CCTV was set up without giving notice, consultation or any information about what was being done with the recordings.
- The court awarded over £17,000 in compensation.

Transparency

6.14 Article 5(1)(a) of the GDPR says that data processing shall be transparent.

On transparency, the ICO says:

> Transparent processing is about being clear, open and honest with people from the start about who you are, how and why you use their personal information, and their rights … You must ensure that you tell people about your processing in a way that is easily accessible and easy to understand. You must use clear and plain language … Articles 13 and 14 of the UK GDPR specify the types of information that you always need to provide people with. We call this 'privacy information'.[17]

16 For judgment, see https://content.next.westlaw.com/practical-law/document/Ib9053153ff5b11e698dc8b09b4f043e0/Scottish-Sheriff-Court-awards-over-17-000-DPA-distress-compensation-for-intrusive-CCTV-and-audio-recordings?viewType=FullText&transitionType=Default&contextData=(sc.Default).

17 ICO, 'Principle (a): Lawfulness, fairness and transparency', https://ico.org.uk/for-organisations/uk-gdpr-guidance-and-resources/data-protection-principles/a-guide-to-the-data-protection-principles/lawfulness-fairness-and-transparency/.

Articles 13 and 14 of the GDPR relate to defendants having to provide information about their data processing in notices such as their website privacy notices.

The claimant should examine the defendant website privacy notice to see if it matches how their data were processed.

If the claimant can show that the processing that was carried out is not mentioned (or is misdescribed) in the defendant's privacy notice, then the claimant may be able to argue that the processing breached the transparency principle.

How easy is it to bring a data protection claim under the transparency principle?

6.15 Claimants will be in a strong position if they can show that the defendants were not open or transparent about the data processing they were doing. Much of this will turn on the facts of the case.

PRINCIPLE 2 – PURPOSE LIMITATION

6.16 Article 5(1)(b) of the GDPR requires that personal data shall be:

> collected for specified, explicit and legitimate purposes and not further processed in a manner that is incompatible with those purposes

'The collection of personal data on any occasion must be for specified, explicit and legitimate purposes … If you want to use personal data for a different purpose from the one you originally collected it for, you need to ensure your new purpose is compatible with your original purpose.'[18]

PRINCIPLE 3 – DATA MINIMISATION

6.17 Article 5(1) of the GDPR requires that personal data shall be:

> adequate, relevant and limited to what is necessary in relation to the purposes for which they are processed ('data minimisation')

Companies should not process more data than they need.

How Easy is it to Bring a Data Protection Claim Under the Data Minimisation Rule?

6.18 Data limitation claims often arises in cases against social media companies. Claimants may allege that social media companies have been collecting and processing excessive amounts data on individuals.

18 ICO, 'What is the second principle', https://ico.org.uk/for-organisations/intelligence-services-processing/principles/#second.

The strengths of these cases turn on the claimant being able to show (a) the purposes of the processing and (b) that the processing was excessive.

Sometimes when a person makes a right to access request under Article 15 of the GDPR, they can see from that that the defendant has been processing excessive data on the person.

Tech companies might be at risk from litigation relating to breach of the data minimisation rule because they often collect and process vast amounts of data on individuals for profiling, tracking and monitoring purposes.

PRINCIPLE 4 – ACCURACY

6.19 Article 5(1)(d) of the GDPR requires that personal data shall be:

> accurate and, where necessary, kept up to date.

Case Law on Accuracy

6.20 In the case of *Aven & Ors v Orbis Business Intelligence Ltd*:[19]

- The claimants were businessmen of Russian or Ukrainian origin.[20]
- The defendants were a consultancy group providing investigative services to clients.
- Buzz feed news published articles in 2017 referring to the dossiers compiled by the defendants about the claimants.[21]
- The court found that the defendants processed inaccurate information about the claimants in these reports.[22]
- The High Court awarded the claimants £18,000 for breach of the accuracy principle under the Data Protection Act 1998 (DPA 1998) as a result of inaccurate data being processed about them. They sued under the DPA 1998 because the breach of the principle happened before the GDPR came into force.

How Easy is it to Bring a Data Protection Claim Under the Accuracy Rule?

6.21 So long as the claimant can prove that the personal data processed were inaccurate and that this caused them damage, they should be able to pursue a claim. They may also have a claim under other laws such as the law of defamation.

19 *Aven & Ors v Orbis Business Intelligence Ltd* [2020] EWHC 1812 (QB).
20 *Ibid*, para 2.
21 *Ibid*, para 4.
22 *Ibid*, para 194.

PRINCIPLE 5 – STORAGE LIMITATION

6.22 Article 5(1)(e) of the GDPR requires that personal data shall be:

> Kept in a form which permits identification of data subjects for no longer than is necessary for the purposes for which the personal data are processed.

How Easy is it to Bring a Data Protection Claim Under the Storage Limitation Rule?

6.23 This may be a challenging principle for claimants. For example, how could a claimant show that the defendant failed to comply with this principle and caused them material or non-material damage?

Secondly, there may be a legitimate reason why the defendant needed to retain the data.

PRINCIPLE 6 – SECURITY

6.23 This principle and the ability to sue for breaches of it are discussed in detail in **Chapter 7**.

PART 2
THE RULES ON MARKETING

6.24 In this section, we consider:

- the main rules on sending marketing communications to people; and
- how breach of the marketing rules can lead to litigation.

AN OVERVIEW OF THE MAIN RULES ON SENDING MARKETING TO PEOPLE

What is Direct Marketing?

6.25 Under section 122(5) of the Data Protection Act 2018, 'direct marketing' means 'the communication (by whatever means) of advertising or marketing material which is directed to particular individuals'.

This includes sending marketing communications to individuals by:

- phone calls;
- texts;
- emails; and

- social media messages.

Direct marketing is advertising or marketing material sent to individuals.

GDPR Considerations in Relation to Marketing

6.26

(1) **People have a right to say they no longer wish to receive marketing material** – this is known as the right to opt out of marketing.[23]

Sometimes, customers say that they do not wish to receive any more marketing material. They may do so by clicking an unsubscribe button at the foot of the email.

(2) **Privacy notices** – customers should be told about how their personal information is used for marketing purposes in privacy notices.

(3) **Lawful basis** – anytime a controller sends marketing to an individual, then it must have a lawful basis in place. If it does not have the individual's consent, then it must have a legitimate interest to market to them.

Specific Rules on Sending Marketing information to Individuals

Email marketing

6.27 The rules on email marketing to individuals such as customers are set out in Regulation 22 of the Privacy and Electronic Communications (EC Directive) Regulations 2003 (SI 2003/2426) (PECR).

Regulation 22 says that companies must have received the prior opt-in consent of individuals before sending marketing emails.[24]

In other words, people must tick a box or do something active in order to agree to marketing. A company cannot assume they want to receive marketing information. There is an exception to this – known as the 'soft opt-in rule'. The rules say that prior opt-in consent for emails is not needed in the following situations:

- Sale – You obtained the customer's email address in the course of a sale or negotiation for a sale.
- Similar products – The marketing relates to similar products or services.
- Opt out – The person is given the chance to unsubscribe from receiving further emails.[25]

23 GDPR, Article 21(2).
24 PECR, Reg 22(2).
25 PECR, Reg 22(3).

Sending marketing emails to personal corporate email addresses

6.28 The GDPR still does apply to sending these kinds of emails to personal corporate email addresses.

Companies sending marketing emails to personal corporate email addresses must:

- tell the person who they are;[26]
- give the person the chance to unsubscribe from receiving further emails;[27] and
- have a legal basis for sending the promotional email under the GDPR, such as legitimate interests. [28]

If we are Relying on Consent to Market then What Kind of Consent is Needed?

6.29 We have set out above the requirements in relation to when consents are needed for marketing. But what kinds of consents are needed in order to send marketing information and what should those consents look like?

Firstly, PECR applies the GDPR standard of consent.

Under the GDPR and PECR, consent[29] must be:

- Freely given – You cannot tell a customer that they must consent or make your services conditional on them consenting.[30]
- Specific – It should be granular. You should not hide the consent in a lot of other terms and conditions.[31]
- Informed – You should give the person enough information so they can make their choice. You should advise them that they can withdraw their consent if they want.[32]
- Clear and plain – Keep it clear so the person knows what they are consenting to.[33]
- Affirmative – The person must actively do something such as ticking a box or saying 'yes' to something to show their consent. You cannot take their consent for granted by ticking the box for the customer.[34]

26 PECR, Reg 23.
27 GDPR, Article 21.
28 GDPR, Article 6.
29 GDPR, Article 4(11).
30 GDPR, Article 7(4).
31 GDPR, Article 7(2).
32 GDPR, Article 4(11).
33 GDPR, Article 7(2).
34 GDPR, Article 4(11).

The company should keep records of the consents it relies on.[35]

Individuals can withdraw their consent at any time.[36] If a company is relying on their consent to market to them and they withdraw their consent, then it must cease marketing to them.

Marketing Emails Cases

6.30 There has been limited litigation for spam email cases although back in 2007, the Edinburgh Sheriff's Court awarded a man £750 for receiving one spam email from the defendants. The plaintiff in that case made a quite persuasive argument on damages when he 'pursued the largest amount available in a small claims case because the Sheriff Court has made judgments before saying that the award of damages should not be so little that it belittles the policy behind the law'.[37]

TAKEAWAYS

6.31

- Breach of the GDPR principles remain a fertile ground in data protection litigation. Often multiple principles are pleaded together to cover the same processing.
- Claimants can claim compensation if a defendant has caused them damage because of infringing of any of the data protection principles:

  (1) lawfulness, fairness and transparency;

  (2) purpose limitation;

  (3) data minimisation;

  (4) accuracy;

  (5) storage limitation;

  (6) integrity and confidentiality (security); and

  (7) accountability.

  Breach of principles 1 and 6 are the most common principles upon which claimants take data protection claims.
- Examples of cases where claimants have successfully sued for breach of the data protection principles include:

35 GDPR, Article 7(1).

36 GDPR, Article 7(3).

37 https://www.pinsentmasons.com/out-law/news/sheriff-awards-damages-of-750-for-single-spam-email.

- *Law Society v Kordowski* – breach of the fairness, lawfulness and transparency principle.
- *Anthony Woolley and Deborah Woolley v Nahib Akbar Or Akram* – breach of the fairness, lawfulness and transparency principle.
- *Aven & Ors v Orbis Business Intelligence Ltd* – breach of the accuracy principle.

• Claimants can sue for breach of the rules on marketing such as when they receive spam emails.

CHAPTER 7

Claims for Breaches of Data Security

INTRODUCTION

7.01 The purpose of this chapter is to consider a particular type of data protection litigation; litigation where claimants sue the defendant because the defendant has either lost their personal data or caused it to be compromised in some way.

This type of litigation is the most common GDPR-related litigation. Whilst there are other forms of GDPR litigation such as claims for breach of the data subject access rules, most GDPR litigation relates to data being lost or stolen.

As we know there are vast numbers of data security incidents. We have seen high-profile data security breaches recently. For example, the Jaguar Land Rover cyber-attack in 2025 will cost an estimated £1.9 billion and is estimated to be the most economically damaging cyber event in UK history.[1]

Companies must report riskier cyber incidents to the Information Commissioner's Office (ICO) under the data breach reporting obligations within the GDPR. The ICO has had 77,221 such incidents reported to it since 2019 – roughly one every 48 minutes for the past seven years.[2]

The most common types of security incidents reported to the ICO in 2025 include:

- data emailed to the incorrect recipient;
- phishing (ie, where criminals trick people into compromising their data security by, for example, scam emails); and
- ransomware (ie, cyber-attacks where criminals use malware (a harmful software) to encrypt an organisation's data and then demand payment for its release).[3]

This chapter considers:

- what the law expects of organisations on data security; in other words, what level of data security are organisations expected to put in place to safeguard personal data;

1 'JLR hack is costliest cyber attack in UK history', BBC News, 22 October 2025.
2 https://ico.org.uk/action-weve-taken/complaints-and-concerns-data-sets/data-security-incident-trends/, p 3.
3 https://ico.org.uk/action-weve-taken/complaints-and-concerns-data-sets/data-security-incident-trends/, p 4.

- what this means for data protection litigation;
- some of the myths that exist around data breach litigation; and
- existing case law on data breaches

PART I
WHAT LEVEL OF SECURITY DOES THE GDPR REQUIRE FOR PERSONAL DATA?

Security Overview Table

7.02

Security breach claims: Chapter summary	
Claims related to breach of the GDPR principle	*In brief*
What is the security principle?	• GDPR expects that organisations process personal data securely and prevent it being lost, stolen or compromised
What is a personal data breach?	• A breach of security leading to the accidental or unlawful destruction, loss, alteration, unauthorised disclosure of, or access to, personal data
What level of security are defendants expected to implement on personal data?	• The GDPR security principle in Article 32 demands that organisations put 'appropriate technical and organisational measures' (ATOMS) in place to keep data safe • Great risk, greater steps – the greater the risk of harm that can be caused by data going into the wild, the more steps need to be taken to protect that data • ATOMS may include technology, such as encryption or organisational steps such as policies or training
What kinds of security breaches claims are we seeing?	As indicated by the cases below, the awards are very variable. We consider data breach cases in more detail at the conclusion of this chapter. Case: *Driver v CPS* • Security breach: Crown Prosecution Service released some of the claimant's details to a member of the public when this was not necessary • Award: £250 Case: *TLT v Home Office* • Security breach: Home Office accidentally published details of people with no right to remain in UK online • Award: £12.5k

THE LEGAL POSITION ON DATA SECURITY BREACHES

7.03 The legislative intent behind the security rules under the GDPR is to say to companies processing personal data that they have a responsibility to make sure it is not accessed by people who shouldn't see it.

Most of the law on data security breaches sits within the GDPR. When data security breaches occur, most claimants sue under the GDPR.

The key security provisions under the GDPR are:

(1) Article 5(1)(f) – This is the security principle, and it says that personal data must be processed securely and that 'appropriate technical and organisational measures' must be used to keep it secure.

(2) Article 32 – This sets out the specific measure that must be used to keep the data secure. It says 'Taking into account the state of the art, the costs of implementation and the nature, scope, context and purposes of processing as well as the risk … the controller and the processor shall implement appropriate technical and organisational measures to ensure a level of security appropriate to the risk'. In other words, having appropriate security in place means companies must have sufficient:

   - cyber security – ie, measures to protect system and devices;
   - organisational security – ie, making sure employees are trained and follow policies;
   - physical security – ie, making sure the building and hardware are safe.

When claimants sue for compensation after a data breach has occurred, they usually include references to breach of Articles 5 and 32 in the letters of claim and pleadings.

WHAT IS A SECURITY BREACH?

7.04 Under the GDPR, Article 4(12) a security breach or personal data breach is:

> a breach of security leading to the accidental or unlawful destruction, loss, alteration, unauthorised disclosure of, or access to, personal data.

Sometimes, it is obvious when there has been a breach of security. For example, if an airline is hacked and the names, addresses and card details of 1,000 customer are accessed by the hackers then that is an obvious data breach.

However, it is not always clear whether a compensable breach of security has occurred. In the case *Farley v Paymaster*[4] some pension statements belonging

4 *Farley v Paymaster* [2025] EWCA Civ 1117.

to police officers were sent to the wrong addresses, but some of the pension statements were returned to the sender unopened. There was a question in those cases about whether a breach of data security had occurred given that the mail had been returned unopened. The Court of Appeal found that 'Proof that the data were disclosed is not an essential ingredient of an allegation of processing or infringement'. But during the case it was not clear whether the court would see this as a data breach[5] as it was not immediately obvious about whether a breach had occurred.

GREATER THE HARM, GREATER THE STEPS

7.05 The security principle can be summed up as follows: the greater the harm that can be caused by data going into the wild, the greater the steps that must be taken to safeguard that data.

The GDPR at Article 5(1)(f) sets out that personal data shall be processed in a manner that ensures *appropriate security* of the personal data. This doesn't mean that security must be perfect.

A risk-based approach is required on security when determining what 'appropriate' security is.[6]

As the ICO puts it:

> The UK GDPR does not define the security measures that you should have in place. It requires you to have a level of security that is 'appropriate' to the risks presented by your processing. You need to consider this in relation to the state of the art and costs of implementation, as well as the nature, scope, context and purpose of your processing.
>
> This reflects both the UK GDPR's risk-based approach, and that there is no 'one size fits all' solution to information security. It means that what's 'appropriate' for you will depend on your own circumstances, the processing you're doing, and the risks it presents to your organisation.

What Does 'Appropriate Security' Mean in Practical Terms?

7.06 This is about the organisation looking at the facts and weighing up the type of security that is needed to keep the data safe.

Deciding whether a defendant had appropriate security in place will be fact- and context-specific.

In deciding whether the defendant had appropriate security in place at the time of the data breach, the court will consider the following factors (GDPR, article 32):

5 *Ibid*, para 6.
6 GDPR, Article 32(2).

- the state of the art – eg, what types of technology could be used currently to keep the data secure;
- the costs of implementation – eg, a court might expect a large tech company to have the best possible security in place to prevent against damaging security incidents;
- the nature, scope, context and purposes of processing – eg, what type of data processing is being done and what is the context; and
- the risk to individuals – eg, the greater the harm to individuals if the data were lost, then the greater the steps needed to keep it secure.

A court could look at these factors and conclude that the defendant did their best in the circumstances and that their security was appropriate despite that fact that security was breached and the data were lost.

What Specific Technology Measures does the GDPR Suggest may be Necessary to Reach Appropriate Security?

7.07 The GDPR does not mandate specific types of technology. Instead, it asks companies to take a risk-based approach when deciding the type of technology to put in place to keep data secure.

Specifically, Article 32 of the GDPR says that proper security may need to include:

- pseudonymisation (temporality removing identifiers from data and storing them separately to keep the data secure);
- encryption (a process that uses a protected key to encode data, ensuring that only those with access rights to the information have the key and can decrypt and tread the information);
- keeping your systems secure and resilient;
- the ability to restore systems after a cyber incident; and
- processes for constantly testing systems.

Is Encryption Mandated under the GDPR?

7.08 Whilst the GDPR is neutral on technology, it does require data to be kept safe. This means that good encryption is often essential.

The ICO says that 'Today, most information transmitted over the internet is encrypted.'

If a data breach occurs and the company has good encryption in place then it may be in a strong position because it can argue that no damage was caused to the claimant.

As an example, in December 2025, the ICO fined a password manager company provider £1.2 million following a data breach that compromised the personal information of up to 1.6 million of its UK users after the hackers got access to the encryption key used by the company to encrypt its data.[7]

Putting the Defendants on the Back Foot

7.09 When data breaches occur and claimants issue proceedings against defendants, the defendants often try to assert that they did have 'appropriate' security in place. For example, the defendants may assert that the breach arose out of a sophisticated hack and there was nothing they could have done.

However, when breaches occur, defendants will have some explaining to do. They should be asked about their security and their encryption.

Claimants should ask the defendants 'what encryption, if any, did you have in place at the time of the attack?' This can put the defendants on the back foot when it comes to defending a claim.

TYPES OF DATA BREACH UPON WHICH CLAIMANTS CAN SUE

7.10 The European Data Protection Board (EDPB) says that data security breaches can happen in three ways:

'1. unauthorised or accidental *access* to data – breach of confidentiality (e.g., hackers accessing the pay slips of all employees of a company);

2. unauthorised or accidental *alteration* of data – breach of integrity (e.g., one employee altering another employee's absence record); and

3. loss of data or *loss* of access to data – breach of availability (e.g. an employer losing the personnel file of one of its employee).'[8]

The author has experience of litigation where an exam provider temporarily lost the names of students on the morning of the exam. The exam provider was sued by one of the students for a breach of the GDPR security provisions and the exam provider paid compensation to an exam candidate.

Does a Breach Always Have to Involve Personal Data?

7.11 Yes. The data compromised must be personal data that can be linked back to the claimant. This is not always as straightforward as it sounds. As we

7 https://ico.org.uk/about-the-ico/media-centre/news-and-blogs/2025/12/password-manager-provider-fined/.

8 https://www.edpb.europa.eu/sme-data-protection-guide/secure-personal-data_en.

know from **Chapter 1**, personal data are 'any information relating to an identified or identifiable natural person'.

For the claim to succeed:

- the defendants must have breached the security rules in the GDPR;
- the claimant must have suffered loss or damage; and
- that damage must have been caused by the breach.

For example, let's say:

- David is employed by Big Company.
- Big Company are hacked by criminals.
- The criminals steal the personnel files of 1,000 employees.
- David's file is one of the personnel files.
- Big Company let David know about the attack.
- However, Big Company have used sophisticated encryption.
- The hackers are unable to break the encryption.
- They are unable to identify David from the encrypted data.
- Whilst a breach has occurred, due to the data being fully encrypted and unintelligible to the hackers, David is unable to prove that he suffered a loss.

WHY IS TERMINOLOGY RELATING TO GDPR BREACHES SO CONFUSING?

7.12 Most data protection claims are brought under the GDPR (and the Data Protection Act 2018). For a claim under those pieces of legislation to succeed, there must be some infringement of those provisions. In other words, there must be a 'breach' of them.

A breach of the GDPR or data protection law can come in many forms, eg:

- a breach of the rules on international transfers (where claimants' data was sent outside UK without a proper control in place);
- a breach of the GDPR, Article 15 data subject access request rules; and
- a breach of the security rules (in GDPR, Articles 5 and 32).

So, when we talk about 'a data security breach' (eg, where data have been lost in breach of the GDPR data security rules), we should be careful to distinguish that from 'a breach of the GDPR' (ie, a breach of any of the other rules in the GDPR).

When speaking about a case where personal data have been lost or compromised, that is a 'data security breach'.

WHAT OTHER CAUSES OF ACTION ARE WE LIKELY TO SEE ALONG WITH SECURITY BREACH LITIGATION?

7.13 The usual suspects are often present in security breach claims when there has been a data breach, ie:

- misuse of personal information (MOPI);
- breach of confidence; and
- breach of the Data Protection Act 2018.

Whether to include these causes of action depends very much on of the facts.

In recent cases, the courts have not been sympathetic to claimants pleading multiple causes of action when they are not made out. For example, in *Smith & Others v TalkTalk Telecom Group plc*,[9] MOPI was unsuccessful. In that case the claimant, a consumer personal information was accessed by hackers. TalkTalk did not misuse his information as there was no positive act.

PREVENTION IS BETTER THAN CURE – WHAT STEPS CAN A COMPANY TAKE TO REDUCE SECURITY RISK?

7.14 To reduce the risk of data security litigation, it is important to have strong data protection controls in place.

This is a vast and very complex area and threat vectors are always shifting particularly with the threat to security posed by artificial intelligence. Below are a few examples of some potential security measures that an organisation might consider to prevent breaches from occurring in the first place.

- **Anonymisation** – If you can anonymise the personal data, then you should do so. The ICO has said: 'In order to be truly anonymised under the UK GDPR, you must strip personal data of sufficient elements that mean the individual can no longer be identified.'
- **Encryption** – The ICOs says 'Encryption is a process that uses a secret key to encode information, ensuring that only those with access to the key can read it. Decryption is the opposite – the secret key decodes the information and makes it useful again.'

9 *Smith & Others v TalkTalk Telecom Group plc* [2022] EWHC 1311 (QB).

- **Pseudonymisation** – ie, taking out identifiers in personal data sets to limit the risk around the personal data processing.
- **Policies** – The GDPR says you must 'implement the appropriate data protection policies' which could include staff policies on data protection and information security.
- **Staff training** – Companies are often targeted by hackers who use social engineering to get unsuspecting employees to click on links which they then use to access company systems.

  These attempts are becoming increasingly sophisticated. For example, hackers are starting to use AI to send fake videos to people to trick them into clicking malicious links.

  Training staff on the risks around data security is vital.
- **Access controls** – Ensure systems are configured in such a way that only those individuals who should be able to see data can access it in practice. Multi-factor authentication should be used where necessary.
- **Technology** – The GDPR expects controllers and processors to consider state-of-the-art technology and to put appropriate controls in place around security, eg:
  - malware protection;
  - incident detection software;
  - data loss prevention (DLP) software; and
  - multi-factor authentication.
- **Physical security** – This area includes ensuring that the building and hardware is sufficiently secure so that threat actors cannot walk on and access information when they shouldn't. The case of *Underwood v Bounty*[10] (relating to a mother and her newborn child's bedside chart being accessed) highlights this.
- **Pen Testing** – Penetration testing is where authorised individuals try to hack into your network to test the robustness of your security controls. It is a vital part of any data security program.
- **Incident response** – Controllers should have a data breach incident response policy to:
  - recognise a data breach when it happens;
  - contain a data breach to stop more data from being lost; and
  - learn lessons from previous data breaches so they do not reoccur.

10 *Underwood v Bounty* [2022] EWHC 888 (QB).

- **Cyber insurance** – It is advisable to ensure that the appropriate level of cyber insurance is in place to cover against data breaches or cyber-attacks. Whilst GDPR fines are usually irrecoverable in the UK, many costs can be covered.

- **Third parties** – Third parties can do untold damage to organisations when they either misbehave with controller data or when they have insufficient security in place.

Target, the US supermarket chain, infamously suffered a data incident in the United States in 2014 which was due to hackers gaining access to its systems through a third-party air conditioning providers sets. The incident was reported to have cost Target $202 million.

PART 2
WHAT DOES THIS MEAN FOR DATA PROTECTION LITIGATION?

7.15 Some potential tips when considering data security litigation: Parties should try to answer the key questions relating to the data breach.

They should consider:

- How did the breach occur?

- Whether the claimants' personal data have been compromised in the attack?

- Were the defendants actually at fault? For example, in the case of *Underwood v Bounty*, the mother of a newly born was in hospital after giving birth. An employee of a company selling baby products entered the hospital and copied some details form a medical chart near the mother's bed. In that case, the court felt that the hospital had not breached her (or her newborn child's) data security rights because hospitals cannot operate without some bedside data, and measures were appropriate.

- What type of data was compromised?

- Was the security sufficient? Security is not cookie cutter. The type of security that is required will spend very much on the circumstances of the case. The more sensitive the data the more the defendants will have to show the security measures they had in place were appropriate.

- Were the data which were compromised encrypted?

The parties may wish to hire forensic IT experts to try to ascertain how the breach occurred and the extent to which the defendants are at fault.

PART 3
MYTH BUSTING

Common Misconception Concerning Litigation Relating to Data Security Breaches

Myth 1 – Claimants can only sue controller defendants

7.16 This is incorrect. If a data processor processing data on behalf of a data controller drops the ball and causes the claimant's data to be lost or compromised, then a claimant can take civil proceedings for compensation against the processor or the controller, or both.

Why might it be more attractive to sue a processor rather than a controller?

7.17 As an example, the claimant may want to sue the processor rather than the controller because the controller may be:

- outside the UK whereas the processor might be in the UK and therefore easier to serve proceedings on; or
- a less attractive financial target than the processor.

Example:

- David is a patient of White Dentistry, a small dental practice in London.
- The dental practice pays a tech giant to host its patient data on the cloud.
- White Dentistry is the controller for the data and the tech giant is the processor.
- The tech giant suffers a ransomware attack and loses David's records.
- White Dentistry tell David about the breach.
- Shortly afterwards, White Dentistry goes into administration due to financial problems.
- David feels that it may be difficult to enforce a judgment against White Dentistry.
- David decides to sue the tech giant for compensation instead of White Dentistry as he feels he is more likely to secure compensation from them.

Myth 2 – If there are multiple parties, it can be difficult to take litigation against them

7.18 This is incorrect. Article 82(4) of the GDPR says 'Where more than one controller or processor … Are … responsible for any damage caused by processing, each controller or processor shall be held liable for the entire damage to ensure effective compensation of the data subject.'

The claimant does not have to prove exactly who is to blame for each aspect of the data processing. Instead, he can sue them all and be compensated. The controllers and processors can fight amongst themselves afterwards about exactly who is responsible for which percentage of the damages.

Myth 3 – Strict liability

7.19

It is wrong to suggest that data claims are strict liability. To succeed in a GDPR claim, the claimant must prove that:

- there was a breach of the GDPR (or other data protection law such as the Data Protection Act 2018);
- the claimant suffered material or non-material damage; and
- the defendant caused this damage.

In *Smith & Others v TalkTalk Telecom Group plc,* the judge said 'the fact that there has been an incident affecting an individual's personal data does not per se mean that the Defendant is legally liable in respect of that incident; there is no such strict liability provided for under the DPA 1998' (or the GDPR).[11]

PART 4
AN EXAMINATION OF SOME RELEVANT DATA SECURITY CASES

Warren v DSG Retail Ltd [2021] EWHC 2168 (QB)

What happened

7.20

- The claimant was a customer who had purchased goods from Curry's PC World (the UK electronics retailer).
- Between July 2017 and April 2018, the defendant, DSG, was hacked.
- The attackers accessed customer personal data including names, addresses, phone numbers, dates of birth, and emails.
- The ICO investigated and concluded DSG had breached the security principle under the Data Protection Act 1998, which requires appropriate technical and organisational measures to protect personal data and it was initially fined £500,000 but this was reduced to £250,000 on appeal.
- The claimant's data was lost and he claimed for:
  - breach of confidence;

11 See para 75 of *Smith & Others v TalkTalk Telecom Group plc* [2022] EWHC 1311 (QB).

- MOPI;
- breach of the Data Protection Act 1998;
- negligence;[12] and
- distress and anxiety from his data being hacked.[13]

Outcome

7.21 The court struck out all the claims, bar the statutory Data Protection Act claim, which was stayed pending DSG's ICO appeal and transferred to the county court.[14]

Why the court decided as it did

7.22

- MOPI and breach of confidence require a positive act of using or disclosing information, not a failure to prevent hacking.[15]
- The court quoted the judgment in *Stadler v Currys*: 'A cause of action in tort for recovery of damages for negligence is not complete unless and until damage has been suffered by the claimant. Some damage, some harm, or some injury must have been caused by the negligence to complete the claimant's cause of action. However, a state of anxiety produced by some negligent act or omission but falling short of a clinically recognisable psychiatric illness does not constitute damage sufficient to complete a tortious cause of action'.[16]

Stadler v Currys Group Ltd [2022] EWHC 160 (QB)

What happened

7.23

- William Stadler was a customer of Currys, an electrical goods retailer.
- The defendant was Curry's the electronics retailer.
- He returned a smart TV for repair in 2020 but did not log out of apps such as Amazon Prime.
- The original TV was resold without a factory reset, exposing Stadler's Amazon account.

12 *Warren v DSG*, para 4.
13 *Ibid*, para 39.
14 *Ibid*, paras 43–44.
15 *Ibid*, paras 22–29.
16 *Ibid*, para 40.

- The new buyer still had the claimant's apps on the TV when he received it and he bought a film when logged into the claimant's Amazon Prime account.
- The claimant claimed for MOPI, breach of confidence, negligence and breach of the GDPR.[17]

Outcome

7.24

- The MOPI, breach of confidence, and negligence claims were struck out; the GDPR claim was transferred to the county court for proportionality.[18]

Why the court decided as it did

7.25

- The court said that disposal of a device without wiping data is not 'misuse' under MOPI or breach of confidence, which require positive use of information.[19]
- It said that the claim in negligence failed because the claimant did not bring a claim for personal injury but sought to recover damages for distress and anxiety. He therefore did not suffer any recoverable loss under negligence, and as a result he has not pleaded a complete cause of action under common law negligence.[20]
- The GDPR claim could proceed but was low-value and more suited to be dealt with in the county court.[21]

TLT & Others v Secretary of State for the Home Department [2016] EWHC 2217 (QB)

What happened

7.26

- The claimants were asylum applicants suing the UK Home Office after a spreadsheet was published online containing their details.

17 *Stadler v Currys Group Ltd*, para 5.
18 *Ibid*, para 5.
Ibid, para 58, 65, 81
19 *Ibid*, paras 56, 58.
20 *Ibid*, para 64.
21 *Ibid*, para 81.

- In October 2013, the Home Office published family returns process statistics on its website. In error it published the personal data of people who did not have leave to remain in the UK.
- The spreadsheet was online for about two weeks and downloaded multiple times, including by unknown third parties.[22]

Outcome

7.27

- Damages were awarded for distress.

  In the cases of two claimants, referred to as TLT and TLU, their circumstances and the 'distress' which they have experienced were comparable and resulted in an identical award.

  The court assessed damages in each of their cases at £12,500.

  This is not out of kilter with awards for moderate psychiatric and psychological damage.

  TLT and TLU felt they had to move out of the area such was their distress about being outed by the document leak.

Underwood v Bounty UK Ltd & Hampshire Hospitals NHS FT [2022] EWHC 888 (QB)

What happened

7.28

- The claimant and her newborn son sued Bounty (a marketing company) and the NHS for MOPI and breach of the Data Protection Act 1998.[23]
- Bounty's business model included collecting data and selling it to third parties.
- Bounty informed the ICO that it shared a total of 35,027,373 personal data records with marketing agencies for the purposes of direct electronic marketing.[24]
- ICO found that Bounty had no legal basis or consent upon which to do this and it fined Bounty £400,000 for unlawful sharing.[25]
- After the birth of the claimant's new born baby, a Bounty rep entered the claimant's curtained bed area at the hospital, looked at the paperwork

22 *TLT & Others v Secretary of State for the Home Department*, paras 1–4.
23 *Underwood v Bounty UK Ltd & Hampshire Hospitals NHS FT*, paras 1–3, 17–20.
24 *Ibid*, para 4.
25 *Ibid*, para 6.

medical chart at the end of her bed and collected it for marketing purposes and sent emails offering photography services.[26]

- The chart had been placed at the end of the claimant's bed and was one of the documents seen by the Bounty representative. The rep used this to get the baby's name and gender.[27]

Outcome

7.29 The claim against Bounty succeeded by default;[28] the claim against the NHS trust was dismissed.[29]

Why the court decided as it did

7.30

- Medical records were securely stored; bedside charts were necessary for care.[30]
- In respect of data protection, the court rejected the submission that, by placing the chart at the end of the claimant's bed the NHS had disseminated or otherwise made available the relevant data.[31]
- The court rejected the claimant's complaint that the second defendant has breached the data protection security principle by failing to prevent the Bounty employee from reading the chart
- MOPI failed because the NHS Trust had no positive act of misuse.

7.31 There was no breach of the security principle by the NHS. Hospitals cannot operate without some bedside data, and measures were appropriate.[32]

Johnson v Eastlight Community Homes Ltd [2021] EWHC 3069 (QB)

Who and what happened

7.32

- The claimant was a tenant of Eastlight Community Homes, a social housing provider.

26 *Ibid*, para 13.
27 *Ibid*, para 38.
28 *Ibid*, para 55.
29 *Ibid*, final section.
30 *Ibid*, paras 33–36.
31 *Ibid*, para 43.
32 *Ibid*, paras 48–49.

- An Eastlight employee emailed another tenant a rent statement but accidentally attached a 6,941-page compilation of other tenants' rent statements, including the claimant's name, email, and payment history.
- The sole recipient immediately phoned Eastlight and deleted the email within hours.
- The inadvertent disclosure therefore was to a single person, who took apparently no issue with it, and lasted less than three hours. The claim was for 'damages for Misuse of Private Information, Breach of Confidence and Negligence, together with damages for breach of Article 8 ECHR rights as incorporated [sic] in the HRA 1998 as well as damages pursuant to Article 82 GDPR and damages pursuant to section 169 of the Data Protection Act 2018.'[33,34]

Outcome

7.33 At para 23, Master Thornett set out that the MOPI, breach of confidence, and Article 8 Human Rights Act 1998 claims were struck out; the GDPR claim was transferred to the county court (small claims).

Why the court decided as it did

7.34

- The breach was minor, quickly contained, and involved one recipient.[35]
- At para 22 of his judgment, Master Thornett asked 'can the *de minimis* principle or *Jameel* apply at least in principle to the GDPR claim?' He went on to say 'Nothing strikes me as distinct in the wording of Article 82(1) of the GDPR as negates continued application (if appropriate) of *Jameel* or *de minimis* principles to a damages claim brought under it.' Master Thornett concluded by saying 'I see no basis for this claim having been issued in the High Court'.[36]

TAKEAWAYS

7.35

- **Regulator judgments** – If there has been a data incident then claimants and defendants should keep an eye on what the ICO has said about it. The ICO often doesn't mince its words or shy away from criticising controllers or processors who have caused data security breaches. If it has fined a

33 *Johnson v Eastlight Community Homes Ltd*, paras 1–3.
34 *Ibid*, para 6.
35 *Ibid*, paras 1–3.
36 *Ibid*, para 24.

company or criticises it, then this can provide useful leverage for claimants to use in settlement negotiations or in court.

- **Security breaches can come in many forms** – Data breach claims usually relate to the claimant's data being accessed by an authorised third party.

  However, they can also include:

  - accidental alteration of data; or
  - accidentally losing claimants' records.

- **Appropriate security** – When a data breach occurs the controller or processor may have serious questions to answer. However, a data breach occurring does not always mean that the defendant is in breach of the GDPR and therefore liable to pay compensation. The defendant may be able to show that they did their level best and rely on the 'appropriate security' defence.

- **Security, security, security** – Prevention is always better than cure when it comes to data security. Security breaches can be very expensive in terms of fines, reputation damage and the costs of mass claims and group litigation. The Target security incident in the US cost the defendant hundreds of millions of dollars. Defendants should take their security seriously at the outset in respect of technical controls, policies, staff training and other compliance measures.

CHAPTER 8

Data Subject Access Request Litigation

INTRODUCTION

8.01 Under UK data protection law, individuals have the right to access and receive a copy of their personal data, and other supplementary information. In this chapter, we consider litigation brought by claimants when companies infringe this right.

The legislative intent behind the data subject access request (DSAR) rules is to allow people to see and challenge how companies process their personal information.

The right to access one's data may be referred to as a DSAR or a subject access request (SAR) or an access request. These terms all mean the same thing.

The author prefers the term 'access requests' or 'DSARs' because the term 'SARs' can sometimes be confused with the separate process for 'suspicious activity reports' (also called 'SARs') under anti-money laundering legislation. Throughout the chapter, we will refer to them as 'access requests'.

Whilst access requests are important in the context of data protection litigation, they are fairly niche so, you may wish to skip this chapter if you have no interest in this aspect of data protection litigation.

The purpose behind the right to access data is to give people the right to see the type of information that companies hold on them.

This chapter looks at the rules on access requests, how access requests can end up in the courts, and case law relating to access requests.

Access Requests – A Legal Minefield?

8.02 Access requests are a legal minefield for organisations. The GDPR and the UK Data User and Access Act 2025 set out the rules under which individuals can access their personal data.

They are procedurally complex and the GDPR sets out rules that controllers must comply with in terms of data subject access requests. In this chapter we will consider those rules and why they can lead to litigation.

The Weaponised Access Request

8.03 There is increasing talk of access requests becoming 'weaponised'. The GDPR has been in force in the UK since 2018. People are increasingly aware of their access request rights. Sometimes people can use the right of access to put pressure on organisations if they are involved in a dispute with that organisation.

For example, if an employee has worked for an organisation for many years, then it can cost the company many thousands of pounds to locate and provide the personal data relating to the data subject.

In *Deer v University of Oxford*,[1] an employee worked for his employer, the defendant in the case, for many years when he made an access request for a copy of his data. The employer had to assess 500,000 emails when collating the data before providing it to the data subject. The access request was reported to have cost the employer £116,000.

Exploding Myths about Access Request Litigation

8.04

- **Myth One – A person can only complain to the Information Commissioner's Office (ICO) if a controller fails to comply with their access request.** False. A person is not obliged to report any matter to the ICO. Individuals are entitled to sue companies which infringe their GDPR rights including the right of access.
- **Myth Two – The Civil Procedure Rules (CPR) take precedence over the access request rules when it comes to the disclosure of documents.** This is incorrect. The access request rules are separate to the CPR rules on disclosure. A person has a right to access their personal data under the GDPR and to receive that data within one month and these rules are not in any way hampered by the CPR rules.

PART I
THE RULES ON ACCESS REQUESTS

What is a Data Subject Access Request (DSAR)?

8.05 A DSAR is a legal right that data subjects have under the GDPR regulation to ask any data controller for a copy of their personal data.

Individuals have certain rights under Article 15 of the GDPR to demand that a controller:

1 *Deer v University of Oxford* [2017] EWCA Civ 121.

- tells them whether it is processing personal data about that individual;
- provide a copy of that personal data; and
- provide certain supplementary information to the data subject to help them understand the data processing. For example, the data subject can ask for information about the countries to which his or her personal data are sent.

For example:

- Rafiq has worked with MegaCorp for 25 years.
- He has recently been made redundant.
- He wants to see copies of the personal data that Mega Corp has amassed on him over that 25-year period.
- He emails his manager and asks for a paper copy of that data. Rafiq has made an access request.
- Rafiq is entitled to access this personal data.
- He is not entitled to non-personal data such as, for example, management information or company financial data that do not relate to him as an individual.

Article 15(3) of the GDPR says that if requested 'The controller shall provide a copy of the personal data undergoing processing.'

Can a company refuse to provide data if they believe the person already has a copy in their possession?

8.06 The controller cannot refuse the request on that basis. Whether or not it believes the person already has the data is irrelevant.

Access Requests – Looking at the Law in More Detail

8.07 Article 15 of the GDPR says that the individual 'shall have the right to obtain from the controller confirmation as to whether or not personal data concerning him or her are being processed'. This is like a gatekeeper request (ie, the individual can write to the controller and ask in the first instance whether personal data are being processed at all).

If personal data are being processed, then the individual can ask for the particulars of that processing.

Article 15(1) goes into some detail about the particulars the data subject can request. They can ask for details about:

- the purposes of the processing (ie, the reason the controller is processing the personal data);

- the categories of personal data concerned (ie, the types of personal data being processed such as name, health information etc);
- the recipients or categories of recipient to whom the personal data have been or will be disclosed, recipients in third countries or international organisations (ie, who did the controller share the data with?);
- where possible, the envisaged period for which the personal data will be stored, or, if not possible, the criteria used to determine that period (ie, how long the personal data are retained);
- the existence of the right to request from the controller rectification or erasure of personal data or restriction of processing of personal data concerning the data subject or to object to such processing (ie, the right to ask for that data to be corrected if it is inaccurate, to ask that the controller stop processing the data in some cases);
- the right to lodge a complaint with a supervisory authority (ie, to complain to the ICO under the UK GDPR);
- where the personal data are not collected from the data subject, any available information as to their source (ie, to clarify details about where the controller got the personal data – this is a very difficult rule for controller to comply with particularly in the context of AI, as we discuss in **Chapter 14**); and
- the existence of automated decision-making, including profiling, referred to in Article 22(1) and (4) and, at least in those cases, meaningful information about the logic involved, as well as the significance and the envisaged consequences of such processing for the data subject (ie, the ability to ask for information about how a computer or an algorithm actually came to its decision).

Is Complying with Access Requests Becoming More Difficult?

8.08 Access requests are a very far-reaching right which give a lot of power to individuals over their personal data. If controllers *'drop the ball'* on any of the categories in the list points above, then the data subject has a right to sue for compensation.

Global companies may find it near-impossible to comply with some of the aspects of Article 15.

With advances in technology companies process more data on individuals than ever before.

For example, AI technology may be trained on data obtained from web scraping. This means that companies developing or using AI may hold vast swathes of data on individuals with whom they have no relationship. As a result, it could be very difficult for that company to find or locate all the data it holds on a particular individual, for example:

- all the sources of the personal data;
- the recipients of the personal data up and down its supply chain if the company has hundreds or even thousands of suppliers; and
- how its AI algorithms work if it is asked for details about that (see Article 15(1)(h)).

Access Litigation – Strategic Considerations

8.09 Defendants in such cases have a range of considerations that may include commercial and pragmatic considerations. For example, it may cost the defendant much more to search their systems and find the data than it would to simply try to settle the case for a modest sum and move on.

Access Requests and the Civil Disclosure Rules

8.10 Access requests are freestanding rights that any data subject can rely on to seek information about how they data are copied as well as copies of that information.

The fact that a data subject may be seeking to get access to their personal data whilst civil proceedings are being contemplated or have been issued is irrelevant to the access request.

In fact, the claimant may indeed be trying to get access to documents by 'the back door' under the access request provisions. In other words, the data subject may be trying to get access to documents to decide whether to issue legal proceedings. They may be using the access request to get documents which they are not yet entitled to under the CPR rules. The Court of Appeal decided in *Dawson-Damer and Ors v Taylor Wessing*[2] that motive is irrelevant. The access request right is a right that sits independently of the civil disclosure rules; it is not curtailed by the disclosure provisions.

Do People Have to Use the Company's Webform to Make an Access Request?

8.11 Access requests can be made in any form. The ICO says: 'There are no formal requirements for a valid request. A person can make a SAR verbally or in writing, including by social media. They can make it to any part of your

2 *Dawson-Damer and Ors v Taylor Wessing* [2017] EWCA Civ 74.

organisation, and they do not have to direct it to a specific person or contact point.'[3]

The author observes that in access request litigation, defendants often complain that the claimant has not used their webform to make an access request. This is a complete red herring as the claimant can make their access request even by tweet or in a phone conversation with the defendant. Of course, from a litigation perspective, it is better to make the request in writing as it is then easier to prove.

To protect against litigation, controllers need to be aware of the ways in which access requests can come in. They need to ensure staff have appropriate training relating to access requests so the organisation can respond to them properly to limit the chances of being sued by a data subject.

Time Limits

8.12 When controllers receive an access request from a claimant, they must fulfil the request 'without undue delay' and at the very least 'within one month'. To reduce the chances of litigation, requests must be dealt within these time frames. This time limit 'may be extended by two further months where necessary, taking into account the complexity and number of requests'.[4]

What if the Person is Making an Access Request to Cause Difficulty to the Controller?

8.13 Controllers can refuse to act on an access request if they are:

- manifestly unfounded; or
- manifestly excessive (see GDPR, Article 12(5).

To rely on these provisions the request must be clearly or obviously unreasonable. Defendants cannot refuse to comply with access requests simply because they are made by challenging or difficult customers. The threshold is much higher than this.

Can Companies ask the Person to Provide ID Before they Comply?

8.14 When handing access requests, defendants can sometimes be dogmatic about ID checks. The author has seen some evidence of defendants claiming that a DSAR was not validly made because a claimant did not provide all the

3 https://ico.org.uk/for-organisations/uk-gdpr-guidance-and-resources/employment/subject-access-request-q-and-as-for-employers/#submit.

4 GDPR, Article 12(3).

ID they asked for as part of their process. However, the controller must try to be reasonable when requesting ID when dealing with an access request. They cannot use the ID rules to get out of complying with the access request.

Under Article 12(6) of the GDPR, defendants may ask for additional information necessary to confirm the identity of a data subject where they have *reasonable doubts* about the identity of the requestor.

Searching...

8.15 We live in a globalised world, where organisations may hold vast amounts of personal data on systems spread across the globe. How far must defendants go in searching their systems for a data subjects' data?

The Data Use and Access Act 2025 (DUAA 2025) sets out that controllers must only make reasonable and proportionate searches when a data subject asks for access to their personal data.

This terminology is still being tested in the courts. Although the case *Deer v University of Oxford* predated the DUAA 2025, the case may be helpful to in determine what 'reasonable and proportionate' mean. Lord Justice Lewison said that 'the result of a search does not necessarily mean that every item of personal data relating to an individual will be retrieved'.

In the context of litigation, defendants should be able to show they conducted a search that is a reasonable and proportionate.

The ICO has said 'To determine whether searches may be unreasonable or disproportionate, you should consider:

- the circumstances of the request
- the volume of information you may need to search in order to respond
- any difficulties involved in finding the information, and
- the fundamental nature of the right of access.'

In terms of resisting litigation, defendants might consider trying to find as much information as they can and keeping records of the searches they conducted so they can show a court in the event of litigation.

Third Party Data – What Happens When we Search for a Person's data, but it is Mixed up with the Data of Another Person?

8.16 The access right is a 'right should not adversely affect the rights or freedoms of others' (GDPR, Recital 63).

The ICO puts it best when it says:

> Most of the time, you should avoid disclosing information about other people. But there may be occasions when the personal data you've pulled together includes information that's closely linked to someone else. ...
>
> First, you should check to see if you need the other person's consent to provide their information. If you don't have the consent of the other person, then you should think about whether it's reasonable to provide that information without their consent.[5]

Litigation considerations: Defendants may be able to refuse to disclose certain information when responding to an access request if doing so would compromise the data protection rights of other individuals. Defendants should consider keeping records of this decision-making process around the third-party data in case the If the access request becomes the subject of litigation.

PART 2
HOW ACCESS REQUESTS CAN END UP IN THE COURTS

If a Person Makes an Access Requests and the Company Doesn't Comply with it, which Remedies can a Person Seek in Court?

8.17 Access requests are a fertile ground for litigation.

If an access request has not been complied with, courts can grant:

- a compliance order compelling the defendant to comply with the access request (A79 GDPR);
- compensation if the failure to comply with the access request causes loss or damage; or
- both a compliance order and compensation.

Remedy 1 – Court order for compliance

8.18 A court can make an order asking the defendant to comply with any access requests that the claimant has made. This right exists under Article 79 of the GDPR which says 'each data subject shall have the right to an effective judicial remedy where he or she considers that his or her rights under GDPR have been infringed'.

Similarly, section 167(2) of the Data Protection Act 2018 says 'A court may make an order for the purposes of securing compliance with the data protection legislation'.

5 https://ico.org.uk/for-organisations/advice-for-small-organisations/subject-access-requests-sar/subject-access-request-advice/#whatshould – ICO Subject Access Request Advice.

The defendant could be ordered to:

- deliver up all of the data they have on the claimant;
- provide a paper copy of that data;
- disclose the details about whether a computer made any decisions about the person;
- disclose details the defendant engaged in profiling of the claimant (profiling is collecting data about the claimant's personality, behaviour, interests and habits to make predictions or decisions about them); and
- disclose details about how an AI model made decisions about the claimant.[6]

Remedy 2 – Compensation

8.19 A court can also order the defendant to pay compensation to the claimant for breach of their DSAR rights. However, the claimant must prove that the failure to comply caused them some form of damage.

Data Access Litigation: An Individual Pursuit

8.20 Data access litigation often seems, as we will see in some examples below, to be litigation taken by individual claimants rather than collective litigation. They do not seem to be the types of litigation that usually lend themselves towards group claims.

PART 3
CASE LAW RELATING TO ACCESS REQUESTS

Bekoe v Mayor and Burgesses of the London Borough of Islington [2023] EWHC 1668 (KB)

8.21 **Court**: High Court

Causes of action: The claimant issued a claim for misuse of private information and breach of his GDPR rights including his GDPR access request rights.

The facts of this case were unusual.

- The claimant rented out properties on behalf of an elderly neighbour called Mrs S who moved into a care home.
- The claimant was appointed as Mrs S's deputy.
- The defendant suspected that the claimant was defrauding Mrs S.

6 GDPR, Article 15(1)(h).

- The defendant began proceedings against the claimant for possession of Mrs S's property.
- The defendant processed information relating to the claimant's finances by accessing it and sharing it during the possession claim.
- The claimant issued a claim for misuse of private information and breach of his GDPR rights.[7]
- In deciding the claimant's GDPR claim, Deputy High Court Judge Susie Alegre found that there was a disproportionate 'access to private information that went well beyond financial information directly related to the letting of the property'.[8]

Access request element: It was found that there was a four-year delay in the defendant responding to the claimant's data DSAR, and the defendant had lost a legal file and failed to provide proper security of his data. This amounted to breaches of Article 5 (GDPR principles), Article 12 (rules around transparency of data) and Article 15 rules on DSAR (para 60). Perhaps somewhat frustratingly, the judgment doesn't say precisely which part of Article 5 was breached.

The court said that: 'The defendant accepts that there were delays in responding to the DSAR from 19 June 2019 … until at least 8 June 2023. This is a significant breach of GDPR with a delay of almost 4 years in responding effectively to a DSAR'.[9]

Result: The claimant was awarded damages of £6,000, including aggravated damages.

Ashley v HMRC [2025] EWHC 134 (KB)

8.22 Court: High Court, King's Bench Division

Causes of action: Breach of Article 15 of the UK GDPR

The facts of the case:

- This is a gargantuan 52-page judgment.
- The claimant was the prominent businessman and former owner of Newcastle Football Club, Mike Ashley.
- The claimant alleged that the defendant breached his subject access rights under Article 15 of the GDPR.

7 *Bekoe v Mayor and Burgesses of the London Borough of Islington*, para 1.
8 *Ibid*, para 49.
9 *Ibid*, para 57.

- The claimant made an access request for access to data that the HMRC held on him through his solicitors in September 2022.[10]
- HMRC accepted that it breached its obligations under Article 15(3) of the UK GDPR in its handling of the DSAR by failing to provide the claimant with copies of his personal data.
- The court held that the defendant's search was also too narrow. They should have searched across multiple departments when trying to locate the claimant's data.
- The court found that HMRC should have searched the Valuation Office Agency (VOA) records right from the start.
- It was not disproportionate for the HMRC to search the VOA records; in fact, HMRC was obliged to do so.[11]
- Mrs Justice Heather Williams DBE said 'I conclude that the valuations (in the VOA records) were Mr Ashley's personal data'.[12]
- The learned judge found that 'it is highly likely that the defendant has taken an unduly restrictive approach to the personal data that it has provided in response to the SAR'.[13]

Explaining the data: The HMRC was required to provide contextual passages or even document extracts so that the data could be understood. This means that merely providing a copy of the data is not enough where contextual information is required[14]

Tax exemption argument fails: The HMRC wanted to rely on a tax exemption relating to DSARs under Sch 2, para 2 of the Data Protection Act 2018. However, Mrs Justice Heather Williams found that any prejudice that the HMRC could have suffered which would have allowed it to reply on that exemption was 'at best, speculative'.[15]

The court said that the defendant remained in breach of its obligations under Article 15 of the GDPR[16] and further that 'the Defendant will need to reconsider its response to the SAR'.[17]

Result: The claimant was successful. The court then invited submissions from the parties on remedies.

10 *Ashley v HMRC*, para 1.
11 *Ibid*, para 194.
12 *Ibid*, para 177.
13 *Ibid*, para 172.
14 *Ibid*, para 211.
15 *Ibid*, para 200.
16 *Ibid*, para 195.
17 *Ibid*, para 213.

Ittihadieh v 5-11 Cheyne Gardens RTM Company Ltd (heard alongside the appeal of *Deer v University of Oxford*) [2017] EWCA Civ 121

8.23 **Court**: Court of Appeal

Causes of action: Claimant sought an injunction and damages for breach of his data protection rights.[18]

This case joined the appeal of *Deer v University of Oxford.*

The facts of the *Ittihadieh* case:

- The claimant, a property owner, had made a DSAR against the defendants as he thought some of the defendants held personal information about him.
- The defendants in the case were directors of a property company and also neighbours of the claimant.[19]
- The defendants claimed that this was a 'fishing expedition and an abuse of process'.[20]
- The court looked at what constitutes a subject access request as well as what is a reasonable and proportionate search

The facts of *Deer v University of Oxford*:

- Dr Deer was an ex-employee of the university.
- She had been in litigation with the university for eight years.[21]
- She made DSARs in 2010 against the university.[22]
- During searches for her data, the university reviewed over 50,000 emails at a cost of £116,116.[23]

Whilst there were several aspects considered by the court (relating to exemptions and other matters), the main salient points concerned the access request element. The Court of Appeal said that just because someone's name is mentioned, it does not mean, without more, that it is personal data.

On searches, Lord Justice Lewison said:

> the implied obligation to search is limited to a reasonable and proportionate search (… it is not an obligation to leave no stone unturned), the result of such a search does not necessarily mean that every item of personal data relating to

18 *Ibid*, para 12.
19 *Ittihadieh v 5-11 Cheyne Gardens RTM Company Ltd* [2017] EWCA Civ 121, para 7.
20 *Ibid*, para 10.
21 *Deer v University of Oxford*, para 15.
22 *Ibid*, para 19.
23 *Ibid*, para 26.

an individual will be retrieved because of such a search. There may be things lurking beneath another stone which has not been turned over. Accordingly, the mere fact that a further and more extensive search reveals further personal data relating to that individual does not entail the proposition that the first search was inadequate.[24]

Result: The court dismissed the appeals brought by Mr Ittahdieh and Dr Deer.

This case was also decided pre-GDPR (the GDPR was not implemented until May 2018). However, it is persuasive about the extent to which searches must be conducted.

Criminal Cases[25]

8.24 Under section 173 of the Data Protection Act 1998, it is a criminal offence 'to alter, deface, block, erase, destroy or conceal information with the intention of preventing disclosure of all or part of the information that the person making the request would have been entitled to receive'.

In 2025, the ICO successfully prosecuted an individual for this offence.

- The director of a care home in Yorkshire, was prosecuted under the criminal law, found guilty and then fined for refusing to respond to a DSAR.
- In April 2023, a woman made an access request.
- She was asking for information on behalf of her father over who she had a power of attorney.
- The director was found to have blocked, erased, or concealed records held by the care home in 2023 to prevent this information being disclosed.
- The personal information requested included incident reports, copies of CCTV footage and notes relating to the requestor's father's care.
- After the director refused to respond to the request, a complaint was made to the ICO.
- During investigation, the director did not provide any explanation about why his organisation would not respond to the SAR.
- At Beverley magistrates' court on Wednesday 3 September 2025, the director was found guilty and was ordered to pay a fine of £1,100 and additional legal costs of £5,440.

24 *Ibid*, para 103.
25 https://ico.org.uk/about-the-ico/media-centre/news-and-blogs/2025/09/care-home-director-found-guilty-of-ignoring-request-for-personal-information/.

TAKEAWAYS

Takeaways for Defendants

8.25

- **Train staff** – To limit the risk of litigation, ensure that staff are properly trained on DSARs so that they know how to respond to them when they come in. Train them on the pitfalls of DSARs including the criminal offences relating to DSARs in section 173 of the Data Protection Act 2018.
- **Staff policies** – Companies should put policies in place around the handling of access requests.
- **Software to find the data** – Put good technology in place to help you find data. GDPR, Recital 63 says 'Where possible, the controller should be able to provide remote access to a secure system which would provide the data subject with direct access to his or her personal data'. If organisations have streamlined processes in place that work efficiently, then they can reduce the risk of streamlined processes – and the risk of litigation.
- **Legal advice** – When dealing with a riskier access request (eg, one relating to an employee on who you hold a substantial amount of data), you may wish to take legal advice so you can comply with it properly.

Takeaways for Claimants

8.26

- **Access rights** – The rules on access requests are stringent. If defendants do not comply, with those rules claimants can apply for a court order requiring defendants to comply with their DSAR. Claimants can also seek compensation if their access request is not complied with in time, although the claimant must prove either material or non-material damage to do this.
- **Court selection** – The Small Claims Track is usually the correct track for a claimant to enforce their GDPR rights.
- **Weaponised access requests?** Access requests can be a powerful tool to use against defendants.

CHAPTER 9

The Tort of Misuse of Private Information

INTRODUCTION

9.01 The purpose of this chapter is to look at two causes of action that often arise in data protection claims. These causes of action are breach of confidence and misuse of private information.

Often these are pleaded along with breach of a data protection statutory duty such as breach of the GDPR or breach of the Data Protection Act 2018.

In this chapter we consider:

- the legal tests for breach of confidence and misuse of private information;
- the advantages and disadvantages of pleading breach of confidence and misuse of private information in data protection claims; and
- the case law where breach of confidence and misuse of private information are pleaded alongside breach of the GDPR.

The table below sets out a summary of the position. The chapter afterwards considers these concepts in more detail.

Related causes of action – Your 5-minute guide		
Topic	*Legal position*	*Comment*
Breach of confidence (BOC)	*Coco v AN Clark* [1969] RPC 41 three-stage test Claimant must prove: (1) quality; (2) circumstances; and (3) unauthorised use.	• BOC is an equitable doctrine • Can be wider than MOPI as can include, for example, trade secrets
Misuse of private information (MOPI)	Two-stage test: (1) Reasonable expectation of privacy? (2) Does freedom of expression outweigh privacy?	• MOPI is a tort • May attract increased damages – see *Spelman v Express Newspapers* [2012] EWHC 355 (QB) (para 114)

Topic	*Legal position*	*Comment*
If claimant succeeds on GDPR and BOC will damages be higher?	If a claimant succeeds on: • MOPI or BOC, and • GDPR claim, will damages increase? Not necessarily. Even if the GDPR and MOPI claim succeed, the court is often inclined to award one pot of damages for the same loss. See *Ali v Chief Constable of Bedfordshire Police* [2023] EWHC 938 – GDPR claim succeeded and damages set at £3k. BOC claim succeeded. However, the award was still £3k	• Claimant lawyers must consider whether it is worth pursuing more than one cause of action.
Remedies available	• GDPR – compensation including material and non-material damages, compliance order • MOPI and BOC – can include injunction, compensation, account of the profits and surrender of the offending material	• See **Chapter 2** for more details on GDPR damages
When BOC and MOPI claims have failed in data breach claims	• In *Warren v DSG Retail Ltd* [2021] EWHC 2168 (QB), the claimant was a customer of the defendant. The defendant hacked and lost the claimant's data. • The court said this was breach of the Data Protection Act 1998. • However, the court said failure to prevent hacking is not a breach of confidence or MOPI – both of which require a positive act.	• Contrast this with *Bekoe v Islington* [2023] EWHC 1668 (KB) where the MOPI claim did succeed (because the defendants did commit a positive act).

PART I
BREACH OF CONFIDENCE

Main Points

9.02 Claimants can take an action under the law on confidentiality for breach of confidence, which I shall interchangeably refer to as 'BOC' for ease of reference.

It is an equitable doctrine[1] and can be used as a means of redress relating to the use of personal information, where that use infringes an obligation of confidence.

1 *Coco v AN Clark (Engineers) Ltd* at 46.

The law relating to breach of confidence can arise in many scenarios including confidentiality relating to:

- intellectual property (eg, where a duty of confidence arises relating to a trade secret);
- contract (eg, where a duty of confidence arises because the claimant and defendant had previously signed a contract such as a non-disclosure agreement); and
- data protection.

This chapter is concerned with BOC claims relating to the obtaining and use of personal information.

What a Claimant must Prove

9.03 The leading case is *Coco v AN Clark* which sets out a three-limb test for proving breach of a duty of confidence.

The plaintiff must prove:

- **quality** – the information has the necessary quality of confidence;
- **circumstances** – the information must have been communicated in circumstances importing an obligation of confidence, and
- **unauthorised use** – there is an unauthorised use of that information to the detriment of the person sharing it.

Let us consider each limb in more detail.

Limb one: quality

9.04 To be confidential, the information must have 'the necessary quality of confidence about it'.[2] If the information is already in the public domain, then a person must have added some thought and effort to existing public domain materials to create confidential information. As Megarry J said in *Coco v Clark*, 'there must be some product of the human brain which suffices to confer a confidential nature upon the information.'[3]

There is a 'reasonable man' test for whether the information was confidential. In *Coco v Clark* Megarry J said 'the circumstances are such that any reasonable man standing in the shoes of the recipient of the information would have realised that upon reasonable grounds the information was being given to him in

2 *Ibid*, at 47.
3 *Ibid*, at 47 line 30.

confidence, then this should suffice to impose upon him the equitable obligation of confidence'.[4]

Limb two: circumstances

9.05 *Coco v Clark* sets out that 'The second requirement is that the information must have been communicated in circumstances importing an obligation of confidence'.[5]

Circumstances which impose an obligation of confidence may arise in three different ways:[6]

(1) **imposed by contract** – one of the most reliable methods of ensuring that information being shared is subject to a duty of confidence is to sign a non-disclosure agreement (NDA);

(2) **implied by circumstance** – do the circumstances suggest a duty of confidence?; and

(3) **implied by special relationship**[7] – the relationship between the person sharing the information and the recipient may also create duty of confidence. For example, the following relationships are likely to imply a duty of confidence:

   - solicitor–client; and
   - employer–employee.

Case study on limb two – implied by circumstance

9.06

- In *De Maudsley v Palumbo and Others*,[8] the High Court considered whether the circumstances had imposed a duty of confidence.
- A man was speaking to other guests at a dinner party.
- He described a night club with novel features that he was going to build.
- One of the other guests took his idea and set up a night club with two of the novel features.
- The court found that the man had not imparted any material qualifying as confidential information and that there was no obligation of confidence on the defendant. The court found that there was an objective test for breach of confidence. Nothing was said by the plaintiff to put the disclosure into a

4 *Ibid*, at 48 line 10.
5 *Ibid*, at 47 line 50
6 Trevor Cooke, 'Protecting Confidential Information – Overview', Practical Law Commercial, Thomson Reuters.
7 *Ibid*.
8 *De Maudsley v Palumbo and Others* [1996] FSR 447.

business as opposed to a social sphere. Also, the idea about the night club was too vague.

- Therefore, the claimant was not owed a duty of confidence.[9]

Limb three: unauthorised use

9.07 There must be an unauthorised use of the information to the detriment of the person communicating it.[10] The defendant must have done something with the information. For example, in *Coco v Clark*, the defendant was alleged to have gone behind the plaintiff's back and used the plaintiff's mechanical design – which the plaintiff provided during talks about whether he would work for the defendant.

Advantages to Pleading Breach of Confidence Claim in a Data Protection Action

9.08 If the facts support it, then the claimant should rely on breach of confidence as a cause of action in a data protection claim. Some courts may award separate damages for each cause of action.

Sometimes courts have felt that it is the breach of the GDPR (or formerly the Data Protection Act 1998) aspect of the claim which should not have been pleaded and that the defendant should have relied instead on breach of confidence on its own.

For example, in *Campbell v MGN Ltd*,[11] Ms Campbell had pleaded two causes of action – breach of confidence (which the court transformed into misuse of private information) as well as a breach of the Data Protection Act 1998. Ms Campbell succeeded in her misuse of private information claim. However, the House of Lords in that case found that the breach of the Data Protection Act 1998 added nothing to the case.

However, it has been said in *Ali v Chief Constable of Bedfordshire Police* that compensation for breaches of European Convention on Human Rights (ECHR) rights does not require the same strict approach to causation of loss as is required for some common law torts.[12]

Disadvantages to Pleading Breach of Confidence Alongside a Breach of GDPR Claim

9.09 Legally, it can be hard to prove the tripartite test.

9 'Breach of confidence', 1 September 1996, Practical Law, Thomson Reuters.
10 *Coco v AN Clark (Engineers) Ltd* [1969] RPC P48.
11 *Campbell v MGN Ltd* [2004] UKHL 22.
12 *Ali v Chief Constable of Bedfordshire Police*, para 54.

If the facts in a data protection claim do not support, it then the claimant should not seek to rely on it as a cause of action. If it is pleaded, then the court must consider it and weigh the legal arguments. If the facts do not support a breach of confidence, then it will only waste the courts time and perhaps aggravate the court.

If a Claimant Succeeds on Liability in a Breach of Confidence and Breach of GDPR Claim, Does that Mean that an Award for Damages will be Made for Each?

9.10 Not necessarily. Sometimes the court will provide a single global figure for both causes of action particularly where it arises out of the same loss or harm.

In *Ali v Chief Constable of Bedfordshire Police*, the claimant Isma Ali telephoned Bedfordshire Police to pass on information about her ex-husband, who she believed was dealing drugs. The report was passed on to the Social Services Department of Luton Borough Council. An employee of that department who happened to be in a relationship with Ms Ali's ex-husband unlawfully accessed and downloaded a copy of the report and passed it to him.[13]

Her claim under the GDPR succeeded. It was held she was entitled to £3,000 under the GDPR. It was also held that the claim for breach of confidence succeeded. However, the award was still £3,000.[14]

There was a similar approach from the court in *Bekoe v London Borough of Islington*[15] where a single figure was awarded for both causes of action.

Where the causes of action overlap, the courts have been inclined to award a single 'collective' figure.[16]

There can be scenarios where the GDPR claim is sufficiently separate from another claim and there could be an argument for separate damages for each cause of action.

For example, imagine:

- A university's systems are compromised and the files of a student called Paul go into the wild.
- The files include details about allegations Paul attending all-night parties during a week when he told the university that he was too ill to attend his exams.

13 *Ibid*, para 1.
14 *Ibid*, para 55.
15 *Bekoe v London Borough of Islington* [2023] EWHC 1668 (KB), para 67.
16 See David Cook and Benjamin Fellows 'Damages awarded for misuse of private information and breaches of the UK GDPR – Bekoe -v- London Borough of Islington', DLA Piper.

- Paul sues under the GDPR because the university breached its GDPR security obligations around his data.
- Paul also sues for misuse of private information.
- He claims he is entitled to separate damages for this over and above the GDPR breach because this contains allegations about his private life (MOPI) which are over and above the loss of security (GDPR).

In BOC cases, the usual award is that the defendant should compensate the claimant for the loss which the defendant has caused. For example, if the defendant used the information to earn profits, then the claimant should receive fair compensation for these lost profits.[17]

Takeaways Regarding Breach of Confidence Claims

9.11

- Breach of confidence is an equitable doctrine – it rests entirely on the court's discretion.
- If a person wants a more reliable way to make information confidential, they should try to get the other party to sign a non-disclosure agreement (NDA).
- Don't throw the kitchen sink at it – only plead breach of confidence alongside a GDPR claim if the facts and the application of the facts to the law support such a claim.

PART 2
MISUSE OF PRIVATE INFORMATION

Introduction

9.12 The misuse of private information (or MOPI) cause of action was created in the Naomi Campbell case (*Campbell v MGN Limited*), which is the key authority in this area.

Misuse of private information is still in its early stages as it was officially recognised as a tort by Tugendhat J in *Vidal-Hall v Google* in 2014.[18]

In *Vidal-Hall v Google* it was decided that misuse of private information and breach of confidentiality are two distinct causes of action.[19]

17 'Protecting confidential information – Overview', Practical Law Commercial, Thomson Reuters.

18 *Vidal- Hall v Google* [2014] EWHC 13 (QB), para 51.

19 *Ibid*, paras 50 and 51.

Misuse of private information was developed to give effect to the privacy rights conferred by Article 8 of the ECHR.[20] Article 8 of the ECHR protects the right to respect for your private life, your family life, your home and your correspondence.

The test for misuse of private information

9.13 There is a two-stage approach for misuse of private information:[21]

- assessing if there is a reasonable expectation of privacy (ie, is ECHR Article 8 satisfied); and if so
- balancing the claimant's Article 8 right to privacy and the defendant's Article 10 right to freedom of expression.[22]

As the court pointed out in the *Campbell* case:

> Article 8(1) recognises the need to respect private and family life. Article 8(2) recognises there are occasions when intrusion into private and family life may be justified. One of these is where the intrusion is necessary for the protection of the rights and freedoms of others. Article 10(1) recognises the importance of freedom of expression.[23]

Determining Whether there was a Reasonable Expectation of Privacy

9.14 The tort of misuse of private information arises out of Article 8 of ECHR which says:

> 'Everyone has the right to respect for his private and family life, his home and his correspondence'.

The Naomi Campbell case

9.15 This is the key case relating to misuse of private information in England and Wales.

The facts were:

- Naomi Campbell took an action for breach of the Data Protection Act 1998 and breach of confidence after the Daily Mirror published photographs of her attending a Narcotics Anonymous meeting.[24]

20 *Vidal-Hall v Google Inc*, Practical Law – Case Digest, Thomson Reuters.
21 Lucy Middleton, 'Privacy Law – key principles derived from the case law', Practical Law, Thomson Reuters. See also *Bloomberg LP (Appellant) v ZXC (Respondent)* [2022] UKSC 5, paras 49 and 56.
22 'Privacy: greater expectations of protection', Practical Law, Thomson Reuters; David Barker, 'Misuse of private information in UK law', 9 May 2023, Pinsent Masons; Henry Hawkesworth, 'Misuse of private information: A tort in its infancy', 23 July 2020, Pump Court Chambers; Lucy Middleton, 'Privacy law overview', Practical Law, Thomson Reuters.
23 *Campbell v MGN Ltd*, para 20.
24 *Ibid*, para 10.

- On 1 February 2001, the 'Mirror' newspaper carried as its first story on its front page a prominent article headed 'Naomi: I am a drug addict'.
- The article was supported on one side by a picture of Miss Campbell as a glamorous model, on the other side by a slightly indistinct picture of a smiling, relaxed Miss Campbell, dressed in baseball cap and jeans, over the caption 'Therapy: Naomi outside meeting'.[25]
- Ms Campbell was awarded of £3,500 in damages in the first instance at the High Court which included her damages for breach of confidence and breach of the Data Protection Act 1998.
- After the Court of Appeal overturned the High Court decision, the House of Lords reinstated the original decision.
- The House of Lords said that Article 8 ECHR and the Human Rights Act 1998 had led to it creating the new action of misuse of private information. The court ruled that the new tort was 'better encapsulated now as misuse of private information'.[26]
- The House of Lords ruled that 'the time has come to recognise that the values enshrined in article 8 and 10.'[27]
- The court found that Naomi Campbell did have an expectation of privacy relating to the Narcotics anonymous meetings.[28]

What claimant must prove

9.16

Is there a Reasonable Expectation of Privacy?

9.17 In determining that the court will look at:

> The question is what a reasonable person of ordinary sensibilities would feel if she was placed in the same position as the claimant and faced with the same publicity.[29]

Is that expectation outweighed by the defendant's right to freedom of expression or other competing rights?

9.18 The court will balance whether the freedom of expression outweighs the claimant's right to privacy. This involves balancing the person's Article 8 right

25 *Ibid*, para 2.
26 *Ibid*, paras 14 and 16.
27 *Campbell v MGN Ltd*, para 17.
28 *Ibid*, para 26.
29 *Murray v Big Pictures (UK) Ltd* [2008] Civ 446, para 35. They quoted directly from *Campbell v MGN*.

to privacy against competing rights such as the Article 10 right to freedom of expression which the other party may enjoy.[30]

Advantages to Pleading MOPI in a Data Protection Claim

Generally

9.19 Strategically, it may make sense to plead more than one cause of action in a claim.

Sometimes a MOPI claim will succeed but the Data Protection Act/GDPR claim will either fail or add nothing to the claim. This was the case in *Campbell v MGN*.[31]

There is no need to prove a confidential relationship to succeed in a MOPI claim.[32]

Increased damages in MOPI cases?

9.20 Also, there may be potential to award significant damages in MOPI cases.

There is very little case law in terms of the assessment of damages in MOPI cases.

In *Spelman v Express Newspapers*[33] the court was considering whether to grant an injunction against the publication of a story about the 17-year-old son of a UK Cabinet Minister.

Tugenhadt J said at para 114:

> If a remedy in damages is to be an effective remedy, then the amount that the court may award must not be subject to too severe a limitation. Recent settlements in the much-publicised phone hacking cases have been reported to be in sums far exceeding what in the past might have been thought to be available to be awarded by the courts. The sums awarded in the early cases such as Campbell were very low. But it can no longer be assumed that damages at those levels are the limit of the court's powers.

The court is saying that it has the power to award significant damages in MOPI cases.

30 Lucy Middleton, 'Privacy Law Overview', Practical Law, Thomson Reuters.
31 *Campbell v MGN Ltd*, para 32.
32 *Ibid*, para 14.
33 *Spelman v Express Newspapers* [2012] EWHC 355 (QB).

Disadvantages to Pleading MOPI in a Data Protection Claim

9.21

- Complexity and unpredictability: MOPI is legally complex in that it often requires consideration of the claimant's Article 8 right to privacy and the defendant's Article 10 Right to freedom of expression. This complexity can make such actions unpredictable.
- Threshold of seriousness: As *Prismall v Google* sets out below, there is a threshold of seriousness for MOPI actions to succeed. *Post-Farley v Postmaster*, there seems to be no serious threshold for GDPR claims although *Farley* is currently being appealed to the Supreme Court.

Remedies Available for BOC and MOPI Claims

9.22 The remedies for BOC and MOPI cases can include various remedies including injunction, compensation, account of the profits and surrender of the offending material.[34]

In BOC cases, the usual award is that the defendant should compensate the claimant for the loss which the defendant has caused. For example, if the defendant used the information to earn profits, then the claimant should receive fair compensation for these lost profits.[35] The position is similar for MOPI cases.[36]

We can contrast this with GDPR cases in which the remedies mainly include:

- Compensation – this includes compensation or material or non-material damage.
- Orders for compliance for GDPR – for example, this could be an order to the controller to cease processing data.

There Must be a Positive Action for Misuse of Private Information Claims

9.23 *Warren v DSG Retail* sets out that '"misuse" may include unintentional use, but it still requires a "use": that is, a positive action'.[37] This means it will be difficult for claimants to be successful in MOPI cases relating to accidental data breach cases such as where a defendant company is hacked, losses information and is then sued by claimants.

34 Lucy Middleton, 'Privacy law overview', Practical Law, Thomson Reuters.

35 Trevor Cook, 'Protecting confidential information – Remedies', Practical Law, Thomson Reuters.

36 Lucy Middleton, 'Privacy law overview', Practical Law, Thomson Reuters.

37 *Warren v DSG Retail Ltd*, para 27.

Pleadings in MOPI and BOC Claims

9.24 In the case of *Stadler v Currys* Lewis J goes into some detail about the pleadings which are expected in MOPI and BOC claims.

He said 'Where privacy and confidence claims are brought in the High Court, CPR PD53B paragraph 8 sets out the information that the claimant is required to specify in the particulars of claim:

For privacy claims, the claimant must specify:

(1) the information as to which the claimant claims to have (or to have had) a reasonable expectation of privacy;

(2) the facts and matters upon which the claimant relies in support of the contention that they had (or have) such a reasonable expectation;

(3) the use (or threatened use) of the information by the defendant which the claimant claims was (or would be) a misuse; and

(4) any facts and matters upon which the claimant relies in support of their contention that their rights not to have the specified information used by the defendant in the way alleged outweighed (or outweigh) any rights of the defendant to use the information in that manner.

For claims for misuse of confidential information or breach of confidence, the claimant must specify in the particulars of claim:

(1) the information said to be confidential;

(2) the facts and matters upon which the claimant relies in support of the contention that it was (or is) confidential information that the defendant held (or holds) under a duty or obligation of confidence;

(3) the use (or threatened use) of the information by the defendant which the claimant claims was (or would be) a misuse of the information or breach of that obligation'.[38]

PART 3
DIFFERENCES BETWEEN MISUSE OF PRIVATE INFORMATION AND BREACH OF CONFIDENCE

9.25

- BOC is an equitable remedy and MOPI is a tort.
- There are different tests, ie, the three-stage BOC test and the two-stage MOPI test.

38 *Stadler v Curry's Group* [2022] EWHC 160 (QB) paras 49 and 50.

- MOPI is still in its infancy, but BOC is very well established over 200 years.[39]
- The author suggests that the key difference is that that breach of confidence can be wider than misuse of private information. For example, breach of confidence can include the breach of confidentiality relating to intellectual property, trade secrets, information that is confidential under contract. MOPI claims only have a privacy element and is therefore a much more specific cause of action.
- In *Bloomberg v ZXC*,[40] the court said that:
  - causes of action for misuse of private information and for beach of confidence are distinct;
  - information may be private but not confidential or confidential but not private; and
  - often breach of confidence and misuse of private information will overlap (ie, if information is confidential, it is likely to support the reasonableness of an expectation of privacy).
- In MOPI claims, the claimant does not have to show that there was a confidential relationship between the claimant and defendant – In the Naomi Campbell case, the House of Lords said that 'the breach of confidence label harks back to the time when the cause of action was based on improper use of information disclosed by one person to another in confidence'. It went on to say that misuse of private information 'has now firmly shaken off the limiting constraint of the need for an initial confidential relationship'.[41]

PART 4
CASE LAW – WHERE MOPI AND BOC ARE PLEADED IN DATA PROTECTION CLAIMS

Warren v DSG Retail Ltd [2021] EWHC 2168 (QB)

9.26

- The claimant was a customer who had purchased goods from Curry's PC World (the infamous UK electronics retailer) and claimed that his name, address, phone number were compromised.
- The defendant was DSG Retail Ltd, the company behind Currys and PC World.[42]
- The defendant was a victim of a cyber-attack.

39 *Coco v AN Clark* at 46 – Megarry J said that the case of *Prince Albert v Strange* (1849) 1 Mac & G. 25 reasserted the doctrine.

40 *Bloomberg v ZXC* [2022] UKSC 5 at para 150.

41 *Campbell v MGN*, paras 13 and 14.

42 *Warren v DSG Retail Ltd*, paras 1–3.

- The attackers accessed customer personal data including names, addresses, phone numbers, dates of birth, and emails.[43]
- The claimant sued for BOC, MOPI and breach of the Data Protection Act 1998 (DPA).
- The court struck out claims for MOPI, BOC, and negligence, leaving only the statutory DPA claim and transferred to the county court.[44]
- MOPI and BOC require a positive act of using or disclosing information, not a failure to prevent hacking.[45]

In TLT & Others v Secretary of State for the Home Department [2016] EWHC 2217 (QB)

9.27

- The claimants were asylum applicants suing the UK Home Office after a spreadsheet was published online containing their details.[46]
- The Home Office admitted liability for misuse of information and breach of the DPA (despite the absence of a positive act necessary for the MOPI claim to succeed).
- The court accepted that damages were recoverable for distress under the common law of misuse of private information in relation to two of the claimants, referred to as TLT and TLU. TLT and TLU felt they had to move out of the area such was their distress about being outed by the document leak.
- The court was of the opinion that TLT and TLU's circumstances and the 'distress' which they experienced, was comparable and should result in an identical award. The court assessed damages in each of their cases at £12,500.

  The case of TLV, daughter of TLT and TLU damages were assessed at £2,500.[47]

Stadler v Curry's Group [2022] EWHC 160 (QB)

9.28

- This was an application brought in the High Court.
- The claimant bought a TV from the defendant.

43 *Ibid*, paras 1–2, 39.
44 *Ibid*, para 44.
45 *Ibid*, paras 22–29.
46 *TLT v Home Office*, paras 1–4.
47 *Ibid*, para 23.

- There were apps on the TV including one which allowed him to purchase movies on Amazon Prime.
- He returned the TV to Curry's without logging out of the apps.
- The defendant sold the TV on without clearing it of his data.
- The claimant brought a claim for breach of the GDPR and the Data Protection Act 2018, misuse of private information, and breach of confidence.
- MOPI – this claim failed because Lewis J said that when Curry's passed the TV to the new buyer it was not aware of the fact that the claimant's information was on the TV. Therefore, it could not have been said to have misused it.

  The BOC claim did not succeed either.[48]

Bekoe v London Borough of Islington [2023] EWHC 1668 (KB)

9.29

- The claimant rented out properties on behalf of an elderly neighbour called Mrs S who moved into a care home.
- The claimant was appointed as Mrs S' deputy.
- The defendant suspected that the claimant was defrauding Mrs S.
- The defendant began proceedings against the claimant for possession of Mrs S' property.
- The defendant processed information relating to the claimant's finances by accessing it and sharing it during the possession claim.
- The claimant issued a claim for MOPI and breach of his GDPR rights.
- Deputy High Court Judge Susie Alegre, found there was a MOPI claim. She stated that 'The defendant has not shown that its interference with Mr Bekoe's Article 8 rights was in accordance with the law and therefore it cannot be described as a lawful and legitimate exercise in the balance of rights … I find the defendant did misuse private information belonging to Mr Bekoe by access details … associated with Mr Bekoe … without lawful authority.'[49]
- The claimant was granted damages in the sum of £6,000 to cover the MOPI claim and the GDPR breaches.[50]

48 *Stadler v Curry's Group*, para 58.
49 *Bekoe v London Borough of Islington*, paras 55 and 56.
50 *Ibid*, para 73.

Prismall v Google UK Ltd and another [2024] EWCA Civ 1516

9.30

- Mr Prismall brought a representative action for the tort of misuse of private information against Google UK and DeepMind.
- The action was on behalf of Mr Prismall and a class of person said to number approximately 1.6 million.[51]
- The claim was for damages of a one-off transfer by the Royal NHS Free Trust of data between 2015 and 2017 to Google and DeepMind who used that data to develop an app called Streams which was intended to be used to identify patients suffering from kidney injury.
- Mr Prismall had extensive treatment at the Royal Free Hospital. He did not consent to his private medical information being collected, transferred, stored or used by Google and DeepMind.[52]
- In October 2015, Google and DeepMind applied to the NHS Research Ethics Committee for approval for a project entitled 'using machine learning to improve prediction of acute kidney injury and general patient deterioration'.[53]
- The High Court struck out the action because the representative class could not establish a reasonable expectations of privacy
- The Court of Appeal said 'We consider that a representative class claim for misuse of private information is always going to be very difficult to bring'.[54]
- The Court of Appeal upheld the High Court's decision: 'This is because we are concerned with the tort of misuse of private information ... The tort involves a threshold of seriousness, and everything will depend on the particular circumstances of the individual case.'[55]

Causes of Action Often Pleaded in Data Protection Actions

9.31 There are numerous other causes of action often pleaded in data protection actions including:

(1) **Breach of contract** – The claimant may assert that the defendant breached a contract between them in relation to the way the data were processed.

(2) **Negligence** – Sometimes negligence is pleaded (ie, that the defendant was negligent in failing to prevent a data breach which caused the claimants personal data to be compromised). It usually does not succeed in a data

51 *Prismall v Google UK Limited and another*, para 1.
52 *Ibid*, para 11.
53 *Ibid*, para 15.
54 *Ibid*, para 66.
55 *Ibid*, para 63.

breach claim as you usually need to show a tangible and material loss such as psychiatric injury.

(3) **The tort of passing off** – Some experts state that the UK may be starting to provide increased protections for the infringements of image rights. See *Irvine v Talksport*[56] where the celebrity racing driver Eddie Irvine's image was used in a brochure showing him listening to a radio with TalkSport on the radio. Mr Irvine was very fast in issuing proceedings against the defendant. He was granted £25,000 damages by the Court of Appeal.

(4) **Breach of other statutes** – For example, under the Privacy and Electronic Communications (EC Directive) Regulations 2003, a claimant might claim that cookies were used to track his behaviour on a website without his consent.

(5) **Breach of image rights**

- In *Douglas and Others v Hello*![57] the actors Michael Douglas and Catherine Zeta Jones signed an exclusive contract with OK magazine for the rights to publish photos of their wedding day in 2000.
- OK paid the Douglases £1 million for exclusive rights to publish the photos of their wedding day.
- However, on their wedding day, a photographer for Hello! (a rival magazine) dressed up as a waiter and secretly took photos of their wedding party.
- Michael Douglas was very annoyed at this. His basic instinct told him that Hello's actions were unfair.
- Ms Zeta Jones felt the situation was an entrapment.
- In the Court of Appeal, the Douglases were awarded £10,800 damages each.[58]

TAKEAWAYS

9.32

- **Risks in pleading multiple causes of action** – If there is an infringement of data protection law, should the claimant seek damages under the GDPR as well as under the law of misuse of private information and breach of confidence? Whether to plead multiple causes of action is highly nuanced question and one that claimants may need to take legal advice on. There is a tendency with many claimants to 'throw the kitchen sink' at a case and to please multiple causes of action on the basis that one might stick. Lawyers sometimes feel they are 'covering their bets' by pleading multiple causes of

56 *Irvine v Talksport* [2003] EWCA Civ 423.
57 *Douglas and Others v Hello*! [2007] UKHL 21, [2005] EWCA Civ 595.
58 See Ruth Boardman and Richard Morgan, *Data Protection Strategy*, 3rd edn, Sweet & Maxwell.

action. However, pleading causes of action such as MOPI or BOC when the facts do not bear them out can be counterproductive. And it can undermine the claimant's credibility with the court. A claimant could be penalised on costs if they plead causes of action that are unsubstantiated. Claimants must be discerning about their best cause of action and proceed with surgical precision.

- **Look at the tests** – The three-stage test for breach of confidence and the two-stage test for misuse of private information can help you understand whether you can substantiate these causes of action in a data protection claim.
- **Positive act** – There must be a positive action on the part of defendants to succeed on a MOPI claim. If a defendant suffers a data breach from a cyber-attack then that defendant is unlikely to be found liable for MOPI (although they may well be liable under the GDPR).

CHAPTER 10

Criminal Cases under Data Protection Law

INTRODUCTION

10.01 In this chapter we will look at:

- the criminal offences under the UK data protection regime;
- criminal prosecutions by the Information Commissioner's Office (ICO);
- how criminal prosecutions may impact civil litigation; and
- how companies can reduce the risks of being involved with criminal offences.

PART I
CRIMINAL OFFENCES UNDER UK DATA PROTECTION LAW

10.02 The UK Data Protection Act 2018 (DPA 2018) sets out the criminal offences under the UK data protection regime. The legislative intent behind the key criminal offences is to deal with the deliberate stealing of or dishonesty around personal information. The law views the theft of information as similar to the theft of physical chattels.

We will look at each offence briefly.

Criminal Offences under the Data Protection Act 2018

10.03

Offence	*Section and maximum penalty*	*Commentary*	*Court*
A. Interfering with the ICO's powers offences			
Intentionally obstructing, or failing to assist with an ICO inspection	• Section 119(6) • Unlimited fine	Defendants can be prosecuted for failing to provide reasonable assistance	Magistrate's court

Knowingly or recklessly giving a false statement to an ICO information notice	• Section 144 • Unlimited fine	When organisations receive an information notice from the ICO, they should be on high alert and ensure the notice is taken seriously	Magistrate's court or Crown Court
Destroying or falsifying information and documents after receiving an ICO information notice	• Section 148 • Unlimited fine	It is a defence if it is proven that the destruction etc would have occurred anyway (ie, in the absence of the organisation being given the notice (see s 148(3))).	Magistrate's court or Crown Court
Intentionally obstructing or failing to assist a person executing an ICO warrant	• Schedule 15, para 15(1) and (2) • Unlimited fine	The ICO's powers are broad. Companies must always co-operate fully with the ICO.	Magistrate's court
B. Blagging offences			
Offence	*Section and maximum penalty*	*Commentary*	*Court*
Blagging or pretending to be someone else, ie: • knowingly or recklessly obtaining or disclosing personal data without the consent of the controller; or • selling (or offering to sell) data if it was obtained in the circumstances above.	• Section 170(1), (4), (5) • Unlimited fine	Defences: see s 170(2) and (3): • preventing crime; • legal obligation; • public interest; • reasonable belief defence; and • journalism.	Magistrate's court or Crown Court

C. Un-anonymising data offence			
Offence	*Section and maximum penalty*	*Commentary*	*Court*
Re-identification of de-identified personal data without consent	• Section 171(1) • Unlimited fine	It is a defence to show the reidentification was for: • preventing crime; • legal obligation; • public interest; and • reasonable belief consent.	Magistrate's court or Crown Court
D. Data subject access request (DSAR) offences			
Offence	**Section and maximum penalty**	**Commentary**	**Court**
Tampering with data in a DSAR It is a criminal offence to interfere with DSAR data by attempting to: • alter; • deface; • block; • erase; • destroy, or • conceal the data.	• Section 173(3) • Unlimited fine	Defences: see s 173 (5). It is a defence if: • alteration would have occurred anyway; and • reasonable belief the data was not disclosable. **Comments:** We saw a criminal prosecution by the ICO on this offence in September 2025 (see *ICO v Blake* below). Quoting this section can be a useful way to get a controller to comply with a DSAR – as long as this is done judiciously.	Magistrate's court
Forcing people to make subject access requests is a criminal offence in connection with employment or the provision of services	• Section 184(1) and (2) • Unlimited fine	Defences: see s 173(5): • preventing crime; • legal obligation; • public interest; and • journalism.	Magistrate's court or Crown Court

LIABILITY OF DIRECTORS

10.04 Section 198(2) of the DPA 2018 applies where:

(a) an offence under this Act has been committed by a body corporate, and

(b) it is proved to have been committed with the consent or connivance of or to be attributable to neglect on the part of—

- a director, manager, secretary or similar officer of the body corporate, or
- a person who was purporting to act in such a capacity.

(2) The director, manager, secretary, officer or person, as well as the body corporate, is guilty of the offence and liable to be proceeded against and punished accordingly.

This means that the ICO could go after individuals in the criminal courts.

A hypothetical example:

- Ben is a junior employee of Dodgy Marketing (Dodgy).
- Dodgy is trying to obtain the details of some NHS patients because it believes it will be able to sell these patient lists to some of its clients in the healthcare sector.
- Jennifer is Head of Marketing at Dodgy.
- Jennifer tells Ben to phone the NHS and pretend to be from the Department of Health in order to secure access to the patient lists.
- Ben agrees to do this.
- When Dodgy obtains the patient lists, it offers them for sale to one of its clients.
- After a whistle-blower complains about Dodgy's marketing practices, the ICO conducts and audits an investigation of Dodgy. Dodgy is prosecuted for 'blagging' offences (ie, falsely trying to obtain personal data by pretending to be someone else).
- Jennifer is also prosecuted under section 198(2) of the DPA 2018 in an individual capacity for conniving to obtain the NHS patient lists.
- Dodgy and Jennifer are convicted in the magistrate's court.

MYTH BUSTER – A PERSON CAN BE JAILED FOR BREACH OF THE GDPR

10.05 This is not correct. A person cannot be imprisoned for breach of the GDPR or the DPA 2018.

However, a person may face a custodial sentence for more serious offences involving personal data under the Computer Misuse Act 1990.

For example, *WM Morrison Supermarkets plc vs Various Claimants*[1] concerned a claim taken by employees of Morrisons in respect of a data breach. An employee of Morrisons downloaded payroll data he was entrusted with at work onto a personal USB stick and took it home. He uploaded the data of 100,000 Morrisons employees onto a file-sharing website and sent it to newspapers He was arrested and convicted of several offences and sentenced to eight years' imprisonment.

PART 2
CRIMINAL CASES

Information Commissioner's Office v Blake[2]

10.06 **Date of conviction**: 3 September 2025

Offence: s 173 of the DPA 2018 (alteration of personal data to prevent disclosure to data subject)

Result: Defendant found guilty by Beverly Magistrate's Court. Ordered to pay fine of £1,100 and additional costs of £5,440.

Fact summary:

- The defendant was director of a care home.
- A lady had power of attorney over her father affairs.
- She made a data subject access request (DSAR) under Article 15 of the GDPR to access her father's data on his behalf.
- She asked for access to incident reports, copies of CCTV footage and notes relating to her father.
- The defendant refused to respond to the DSAR.
- The defendant was found to have 'to have blocked, erased, or concealed records … between 12 April and 12 May 2023 to prevent this information being disclosed.'
- When the defendant refused to respond to the DSAR, a complaint was made to the ICO.
- When the ICO investigated, it appeared that the defendant did not help his position by refusing to provide any explanation about why he would not respond to the DSAR.

1 *WM Morrison Supermarkets plc vs Various Claimants* [2020] UKSC 12.

2 https://ico.org.uk/about-the-ico/media-centre/news-and-blogs/2025/09/care-home-director-found-guilty-of-ignoring-request-for-personal-information/.

Information Commissioner's Office v Saleem[3]

10.07 Date of conviction: 16 May 2024

Offence: Unlawfully accessing personal data under s170 of the Data Protection Act 2018

Result: Defendant found guilty by Huddersfield Magistrate's Court. Ordered to pay fine of £265 and additional costs of £450.

Fact summary:

- The defendant was a trainee manager at a UK branch of a well-known car rental firm.
- The defendant came into work outside his scheduled hours one Sunday.
- An internal audit at the firm at which he worked found that he accessed customer data.
- The defendant was found to have unlawfully accessed 213 records with personal data during dates in 2019.
- He was dismissed by his employers.
- The car hire company referred the case to the ICO.
- The ICO later said that 'Unfortunately, these incidents cannot always be avoided due to some people having malign intent. Organisations can, however, put measures in place to mitigate occurrences by, as Enterprise Rent-A-Car did, having internal audit arrangements in place and ensuring staff are educated about data protection and information governance responsibilities, and how to handle people's data responsibly.'

Information Commissioner's Office v Riches[4]

10.08 Date of conviction: August 2024

Offence: s 55 of Data Protection Act 1998

Result: Defendant pleaded guilty at Cardiff Crown Court. Ordered to pay fine of £10,000 and additional costs of £1,700.

Fact summary:

- The defendant was prosecuted under the GDPR-type regime in existence under the Data Protection Act 1998 as the offences occurred back in 2009 to 2011.

3 https://ico.org.uk/about-the-ico/media-centre/news-and-blogs/2024/05/car-rental-manager-fined-after-unlawfully-obtaining-customer-data/.

4 https://ico.org.uk/about-the-ico/media-centre/news-and-blogs/2024/08/porthcawl-man-sentenced-after-brazen-car-scam-worth-hundreds-of-thousands-of-pounds/.

- The defendant was an employee of a car hire firm.
- The defendant left to set up his own personal injury company, but he stayed in touch with his former colleagues at the car rental firm.
- The employees at his former employer company illegally passed information to him which he would use in his new business venture.
- His former employer managed to obtain a £300,000 civil judgment against the defendant but at that point he had absconded to the USA.
- He was subject to an arrest warrant, and he surrendered himself to the authorities in 2024.
- The ICO described Riche's actions as a 'brazen operation'.
- The ICO said that the (perhaps appropriately named) Mr Riches accessed his former employer's systems 'to steal data which he then used to enrich himself to the tune of hundreds of thousands of pounds'.

Information Commissioner's Office v Okparavero & Islam[5]

10.09 **Date of conviction**: 8 October 2024

Offence: Offences under the Computer Misuse Act 1990 and DPA 2018

Result: Defendants pleaded guilty at Minshull Street Court (Manchester). Sentenced to six-month prison sentence (suspended 18 months). Each were ordered to complete 150 hours of unpaid work.

Fact summary:

- The defendants worked at RAC call centres.
- They unlawfully copied and sold 'over 29,500 lines of personal information'.
- Their behaviour was discovered and reported to the RAC.
- After phones were seized, it showed that the defendants had been paid by a third party to sell the information.
- The RAC told the ICO about it.
- The ICO said to 'take steps to profit from other people's misfortune by selling that information is appalling.'

5 https://ico.org.uk/about-the-ico/media-centre/news-and-blogs/2024/10/criminal-record-and-suspended-prison-sentence-handed-to-former-rac-employees/.

PUBLICITY FOR CRIMINAL OFFENCES

10.10 The negative publicity that can ensue form a criminal conviction relating to any of the offences above can be significant. These cases are often reported in the press.

Criminal offences under the DPA 2018 are recordable offences – this means they will be kept on police records (s 199).

WHO BRINGS THE PROSECUTIONS?

10.11 This is set out at section 197 of the DPA 2018. Offences under the DPA 2018 are brought by the ICO with the consent of the Director of Public Prosecutions (or the Director of Public Prosecutions for Northern Ireland in Northern Ireland).[6]

IMPACT ON CIVIL LITIGATION – COULD CRIMINAL PROCEEDINGS PUT PRESSURE ON THE DEFENDANTS TO SETTLE CIVIL CASES?

10.12 As we know, a person can sue for damages if there has been an infringement of their data protection rights under the GDPR and the DPA 2018.

Sometimes the conduct upon which the data subject is founding a civil action can also be a criminal offence. For example, it is a criminal offence to delete data to prevent it from being released as part of a subject access request. A defendant may also issue a civil claim on the basis that the subject access request was mishandled. The spectre of potential criminal proceedings could sometimes concentrate the defendants' minds and encourage them to 'settle up' quickly and ensure any settlement agreement is subject to a confidentiality clause.

However, it is advisable that one must be extremely careful about this and to only make allegations of potential criminal conduct relating to offences under the DPA 2018 (or any other statute) when there is a basis for doing so.

TAKEAWAYS

10.13

- **Data protection training** – Staff members in companies should receive data protection training so they understand their data protection responsibilities and are familiar with the risks around data protection including the criminal offences under data protection law.

6 Section 197 sets out that in relation to proceedings in Scotland, section 136(3) of the Criminal Procedure (Scotland) Act 1995 (deemed date of commencement of proceedings) applies for the purposes of this section as it applies for the purposes of that section.

- **Technical controls** – Appropriate information security controls should be in place to prevent staff members from stealing information or sending it outside the company. For example, software can be installed to prevent large amounts of data from being sent outside the company.
- **Personal liability** – Management should be made aware of the personal liability offences. Individuals can be prosecuted in an individual capacity for some data protection offences.

CHAPTER 11

Commercial Litigation when a Technology Supplier Causes a Data Incident

INTRODUCTION

11.01 This chapter is different from the other chapters in this book. In the other chapters, we consider data protection litigation instigated by individuals for breach of their data protection rights and freedoms.

In this chapter we consider commercial litigation (ie, data protection litigation between corporate entities). Specifically, we examine data protection litigation which arises when a company sues a technology provider. A tech provider is a third party that supplies IT systems of digital services that process data on a company's behalf. This could include things like software solutions, IT services or cloud technology. Different names might be used to describe these providers – supplier, vendor, service provider – in this chapter we use the term technology provider. We discuss the legal ramifications of one company entrusting another company to process their data. Such litigation can be complex and this chapter does not have all the answers. However, the chapter should serve as an introduction to such litigation.

Commercial data protection litigation is becoming more common.

There are numerous reasons for this including:

- the increasing reliance on suppliers for tasks that corporates used to perform in house;
- the proliferation of new supplier technology (such as AI and cloud software) which can cause large scale data incidents when it malfunctions; and
- the increase in cyber-attacks as hackers try and access the data in supplier systems for ransomware attacks.

From a legal perspective, much of the commercial litigation relating to personal data is underpinned by Article 28 of the GDPR. The purpose behind Article 28 is to stop organisations outsourcing their data processing and then trying to pin the blame on their supplier when the supplier mishandles the data.

Is Technology Provider Litigation the Only Type of Commercial Data Protection Litigation which can Arise Between Companies?

11.02 No, there are multiple types of commercial data litigation.

However, in this chapter we focus on one of the more prominent types of commercial data protection litigation scenarios that arise when:

- a business (which is a controller for the personal data),
- hires a supplier (which is a processor for that data), and
- that supplier then causes a data breach.

Why does this Lead to Commercial Data Protection Litigation Between Companies?

11.03 The first reason is that businesses hand over their employee and customer personal data to these suppliers. The suppliers need access to the data to perform their services. And when the supplier fails and that data is compromised that leads to litigation. When technology providers cause a data breach it can be very expensive.

For example, a supplier of file transfer software which was used to move sensitive data over the internet was hacked in 2023. This hack reportedly affected over 1,000 businesses. The cost of the hack was reported to be $9.923 billion.[1]

CHAPTER SUMMARY TABLE

11.04

Chapter summary: Commercial litigation when a technology provider causes a data incident	
Topic	*In brief*
Why technology provider breaches lead to commercial litigation?	• Businesses often give their technology providers access to their personal data. • When these technology providers are hacked that can lead to massive commercial, reputational and regulatory damage for businesses. • The business must consider whether it can sue the technology provider to recover some of the loss.

1 'MOVEit, the biggest hack of the year, by the numbers', https://techcrunch.com/2023/08/25/moveit-mass-hack-by-the-numbers/.

Topic	*In brief*
What is usually in the contract?	• The clauses usually include obligations on the: o services; o confidentiality; o security requirements – crucial clauses when dealing with technology providers; o data breach requirements; and o indemnities for losses.
Indemnity clauses	• An indemnity is a promise by the supplier to compensate the loss if a data breach happens. • Commercial litigation against technology providers often succeeds or fails on these clauses.
Actions for claimants or defendants if a technology provider has suffered a data breach	• act quickly • gather facts • assess evidence • consider contract • get specialist legal advice • try to preserve privilege on key documents

Structure of the Chapter

11.05 This chapter is divided into four parts:

- Part 1 – provides an overview of litigation against a technology provider.
- Part 2 – provides an examination of the clauses likely to appear in a contract against a technology provider.
- Part 3 – provides consideration of some Information Commissioner's Office (ICO) enforcement against technology providers.
- Part 4 – outlines some steps that claimants can take to maximise their position in litigation against a supplier, as well as some steps that defendants can take to maximise their position.

PART 1
AN OVERVIEW OF LITIGATION AGAINST A TECHNOLOGY PROVIDER

What is a Technology Provider?

11.06 A technology provider is an external service provider that provides information technology services to companies and other organisations to businesses and organisations. These services often include the provision of software, cloud services, and technical support. Suppliers are sometimes referred to as vendors, third party vendors, or even processors. I will refer to them as 'suppliers'. I refer to the other party to the contract (the party which has hired the supplier) as either 'the business' or 'the controller'.

What is a Data Breach?

11.07 Under the GDPR a data breach occurs 'whenever any personal data is accidentally lost, destroyed, corrupted or disclosed; if someone accesses the data or passes it on without proper authorisation; or if the data is made unavailable and this unavailability has a significant negative effect on individuals'.[2]

Are Technology Providers the Main Cause of Data Breaches?

11.08 Many reports suggest that human error is the main cause of data breaches. For example, when an employee clicks on a malicious link that can cause a data breach.[3] However, many reports suggest that supplier failure is one of the most common causes of large-scale data breaches.

PART 2
CONTRACT IS KING – EXAMINING THE CLAUSES LIKELY TO APPEAR IN A CONTRACT WITH A TECHNOLOGY PROVIDER

Introduction

11.09 Sometimes technology providers are responsible for data breaches. Whether the claimant business is successful in taking a claim against the technology provider depends on the contract between the parties. In this chapter we consider the types of clauses that usually appear in contracts for outsourced IT services. We consider their importance in commercial data protection litigation.

Often the technology provider is sued for negligence was well as breach of contract. However, the main thrust of the action will usually centre around the breach of contract claim. The claim may include various aspects such as:

- breach of express terms of the contract – eg, that the supplier would notify the business of a data breach with 24 hours;
- breach of implied terms – eg, that the supplier would take reasonable care and skill in safeguarding the data;
- breach of warranty – eg, that the supplier gave a warranty that they had specific security standards; and
- misrepresentation – eg, that the supplier dishonestly claimed they had no history of data breaches.

2 ICO, Personal Data Breaches: A Guide, https://ico.org.uk/for-organisations/report-a-breach/personal-data-breach/personal-data-breaches-a-guide/.

3 ICO, Data Security Incidents Trends. Data Security Incidents Dashboard, https://ico.org.uk/action-weve-taken/complaints-and-concerns-data-sets/data-security-incident-trends/, p 4.

What Kind of Losses does a Business Usually Seek when it Sues a Technology Provider?

11.10 When a data breach occurs the business often sues its supplier for multiple, different types of loss, for example:

- direct losses – eg, containment and clean-up costs following the data breach;
- regulator losses – losses relating to regulatory fines, audits and investigations;
- claims from individuals – the loss the businesses suffered because of being sued by their customers whose data was affected by the breach; and
- operational losses – eg, loses relating to the businesses systems being affected which prevented their business from accessing their services.

Is there much Case Law Relating to Technology Provider Failing?

11.11 No. It is likely that many of these cases settle before trial. Often the technology providers want to avoid any adverse publicity.

Considering the Contract Between the Controller and the Technology Provider

11.12 In some cases, there will be no written contract between the business and the supplier. That may mean that the court must decide what the agreement was between the controller and the technology provider through a 'course of dealing'. However, in most cases there is a written contract in place. Litigation between businesses and suppliers is usually based of the contract between those entities.

The potential merits or demerits of that litigation will usually depend on the clauses within that contract. As with other areas of data protection legislation, the devil is often in the detail.

Which Clauses are Likely to be in a Technology Provider Contract?

11.13

The usual suspects – clauses that usually appear in a contract with a technology provider			
Clause	*Overview*	*Mandated by the GDPR?*	*Why might these clauses be relevant when a business sues their supplier after a data breach?*
1. Description of services	These clauses should be clear about the services the supplier is providing, the type of data.	Yes. Mandated where a controller hires a technology provider processor. See Article 28 of the GDPR.	When a data breach happens suppliers often try to escape liability by claiming that the loss arose outside the services they agreed to deliver.
2. Security	These clauses set out the technical (eg, encryption) and organisational (eg, staff training) security measures that the technology provider must take to ensure the security of any personal data.	Yes. As above.	This is the focal point of the contract in litigation against a technology provider. Did the supplier breach the security measures in the contract? Consider the clauses very carefully to see if the supplier met the requirements.
3. Defendant staff will keep data confidential	Clauses setting out how the technology provider staff are required to keep the data confidential.	Yes. As above.	It is easier to sue a supplier where their staff are subject to specific obligations.
4. Sub suppliers	These clauses govern whether the technology provider can sub-contract out the services to their own sub suppliers.	Yes. As above.	Security is only as strong as the weakest link in the supply chain. Was the breach caused by the technology provider using a dodgy sub supplier?

Clause	*Overview*	*Mandated by the GDPR?*	*Why might these clauses be relevant when a business sues their supplier after a data breach?*
5. Audit rights	These clauses set out how the business can audit the supplier's systems.	Yes. As above.	If a breach occurs and there are strong audit rights in the contract, the business may ask the supplier to provide reports relating to the breach.
6. Data subject rights	Individuals have certain rights over their personal data under the GDPR (eg, the right of access). The supplier may have to help the business comply with these rights.	Yes. As above.	These clauses are not usually important in technology provider litigation.
7. Supplier obligations to notify business of data breaches	The business must be told about breaches of their data by their technology provider. Some businesses require immediate notification or notification within 24 hours.	Yes. As above.	If a technology provider causes a data breach the business will want to be told of the breach very quickly. If the supplier delays in notifying, it might cause the business more loss and damage.
8. Deleting the data at the end of the contract	These clauses say what will happen to the personal data at the end of the contract.	Yes. As above.	These clauses are not usually important in technology provider litigation
9. Limitation of liability and indemnity clauses	See full explanation in the commentary below.	*Not* mandated by the GDPR.	These clauses set out the extent to which any losses may be recovered if the technology provider is responsible for a data breach of the businesses data. This is often where the litigation is won or lost. GDPR fines may not be recoverable in the UK (see below).

Limitation of Liabilities and Indemnity

11.14 These clauses allow the business to recover any losses if the technology provider is responsible for a data breach of the businesses data.

These clauses are very important in managing risk.

The business will want the supplier to includes indemnities or warranties in the contract to cover any loss and damage they sustain because of the supplier's breach of the contract.

Indemnity

11.15 An indemnity 'is a promise by the party giving the indemnity (paying party) to protect the beneficiary of the indemnity (receiving party) against an identified loss by paying money if a special trigger event occurs … It is widely considered that an indemnity gives quicker, easier and fuller recovery than other claims.'[4]

The business will look carefully at how the indemnity is worded. If it is comprehensive and it covers all direct and indirect loses and it spells out and gives details about those recoverable losses, then the customer will be in a strong position. If the indemnity is more narrowly drafted then the supplier may be arguing that their obligations to provide cover for the loss is minimal.

An indemnity claim can be easier to prove than a breach of contract claim because the customer need only prove:

- the loss occurred; and
- trigger event occurred.[5]

Often the business will be saying that the indemnity clause covers all the loss it sustained. Conversely, the supplier will say the indemnity only covers very limited losses.

Warranty

11.16 A warranty is 'an assurance or a promise in a contract, the breach of which may give rise to a claim in damages'.[6] With warranties, the claimant has a higher bar to reach than proving a breach of an indemnity. When claiming for a breach of warranty the claimant must prove the breach of the warranty as well as loss and causation etc.

4 'Contracts: Indemnities', Practical Law, Thomson Reuters.

5 Data Processing Agreements – Executive Editor – Justin B Weiss – IAPP – Chpt 6 – Dyson, Craddock Van Ecke and Lazenby

6 'Glossary: Warranty', Practical Law, Thomson Reuters.

Limitation of liability clause

11.17 A limitation of liability clause is 'a clause in a commercial agreement which allows parties to apportion risk or exclude liability between themselves for certain types of default under the contract.'[7]

Before contemplating issuing or defending data protection litigation, look carefully at any indemnities, warranties or limitations in the contract.

Is this mandated under the GDPR? No, liability and indemnity clauses are not mandated under the GDPR.

Can Contracts Cover GDPR Fines?

11.18 Sometimes businesses ask their suppliers to include clauses in the contact saying that the supplier will cover the cost of any GDPR fines that the business faces if the GDPR breach is caused by the supplier. These clauses are generally unenforceable in UK law as UK courts disapprove of organisations trying to outsource these fines. They want companies that receive such fines to feel the financial pain of having to pay the fine themselves.

The Future of Data Protection Contracts

11.19 When a controller contracts with a processor who is processing data on behalf of the controller, then the GDPR clauses set out in the table at para **11.13** in the chapter are mandatory.

There is a trend for more regulations mandating clauses with suppliers. For example, the EU Digital Operational Resilience Act (DORA) – which can apply to UK suppliers to EU financial entities – also mandates certain supplier clauses.

PART 3
CONSIDERATION OF SOME ICO ENFORCEMENT DECISIONS AGAINST TECHNOLOGY PROVIDERS

Technology Provider Drops the Ball Causing Damage and Loss to the NHS[8]

11.20

- In March 2025, the ICO fined a technology provider (Advanced Computer Software Group Ltd) £3.07 million. Advanced Computer Software Group Ltd provides IT and software services to organisations on a national scale.

7 Dyson, Craddock Van Ecke and Lazenby, 'Data Processing Agreements', Justin B Weiss (exec ed), IAPP, Ch 6.

8 https://ico.org.uk/about-the-ico/media-centre/news-and-blogs/2024/08/provisional-decision-to-impose-6m-fine-on-software-provider-following-2022-ransomware-attack/.

- The IT provider acted as a processor for the NHS. It provided IT and software services to the NHS.
- During a ransomware incident, hackers accessed several of the technology provider's health care systems via a customer account that should have been protected with multi factor authentication but did not have it.
- The data of 80,000 people was compromised due to the attack.
- There was 'disruption to critical services such as NHS 111, and other healthcare staff unable to access patient records.'

Ticketmaster Supplier Loses Data but Ticketmaster Received the Fine[9]

11.21

- Ticketmaster's technology provider caused a data breach.
- Ticketmaster was fined £1.25 million in 2020.
- Ticketmaster had hired a technology provider who provided it with chat bot technology for its website.
- A hacker was able to use the chatbot to access customer payment details.
- As a result, it was reported that many thousands of people were victims of fraud.
- Ticketmaster was sued by many of its customers as a result.
- Ticketmaster later appealed the fine but dropped the appeal.

PART 4
STEPS THAT CLAIMANTS OR DEFENDANTS CAN TAKE TO MAXIMISE THEIR POSITION IN LITIGATION

11.22 This section covers the steps that business can take to prepare for litigation against their suppliers in the event that one of their suppliers is hacked.

See **Chapter 7** on security if you want more information relating to individuals taking claims against companies when there has been a breach of security.

STEPS CLAIMANTS CAN TAKE

11.23 Often businesses will feel that a supplier with whom they have a contract has dropped the ball and caused loss or damage to the controller. For example, the

9 https://www.bbc.co.uk/news/technology-54931873.

supplier may have been the victims of a cyber-attack which caused the business's data to be lost as per the example of the ICO action above.

Or, perhaps the one of the supplier's employees has stolen the data and sold it on the dark web.

How was the Breach Caused

11.24 The business should get out in front of the facts and try to determine how the breach was caused.

It might not always be easy to determine how personal data went out in to the wild. For example:

- Was it a supplier system failure?
- Was the supplier hacked?
- Did one of the supplier's employees cause the data breach?

It is crucial to ascertain how the breach was caused if the business wants to establish liability against the supplier.

The business must assess the specific facts of the case and the alleged breach.

Speed is the most important factor in gathering facts and preserving evidence.

If necessary, hire forensic IT investigators to find out how the breach occurred.

The Strength of the Evidence

11.25 The business will need to assess the relevant documents, eg:

- logs;
- forensic IT reports; and
- the timelines on when and how the breach happened.

Usually, cases between corporates will relate to breaches of security (ie, where data has been compromised or lost by the supplier).

The evidence upon which the claimant can rely upon which to base a claim will vary from case to case.

The business should try to gather as much evidence as it can to assist in its case against the supplier.

Documents, notifications form the supplier, the contract, logs are crucial in building the case.

The Contract

11.26 The business should consider the contract and related documentation in detail.

Are there liabilities and indemnities upon which the business can rely to cover any losses related to the breach?

How clear is it that the supplier is in breach of the contract?

Specialist Legal Advice

11.27 The business should consider obtaining specialist legal advice on the strength of their case.

ICO Enforcement against the Supplier

11.28 The ICO can reprimand, fines or even prosecutes entities for breach of the GDPR.

Monitor any potential enforcement action by the ICO against the supplier carefully.

If the supplier is fined by the ICO then this will likely bolster the business's case against the supplier.

Commercial Considerations

11.29 Consider whether the supplier/processor has deep pockets and can cover the costs of the breach of the contract

Decide on Appropriate Remedy

11.30 The business may be seeking damages for all the losses incurred as a result of the data breach. Alternatively, it may be seeking other remedies such as, for example:

- an injunction (eg, on the basis that the data be returned or deleted); or

- a declaration (eg, on the basis that the business was in no way at fault).

Set Litigation Strategy

11.31 The business will have to decide on the best strategy based on the legal, commercial and practical considerations.

For example, it may wish to incur a minimum about of publicity.

Notify Insurers

11.32 The business should let its cyber insurers know about the breach immediately as delaying notification may jeopardise the cover.

STEPS DEFENDANTS CAN TAKE

Gather Facts

11.33 In terms of gathering the facts, defendants will be in a more advantageous position than claimants given that the breach is likely to have occurred on their own systems.

They can get specialist help from forensic IT experts on the breach which will allow them to see what the causes of the breach were.

Was there any contributory negligence on the part of the business?

What were the timelines in terms of how the breach occurred?

Advise stakeholders not to put anything in writing if they can avoid it.

Chain of Causation

11.34 Can the defendants show that the breach was not caused by the supplier's acts or omissions?

The Strength of the Evidence

11.35 Preserve any logs, reports internal documents that may show how the breach occurred as well as the extent of the loss.

The Contract

11.36 The supplier should consider the contract and related documentation in detail.

Are there any clauses within the contract that work to the supplier's advantage in terms of the breach?

For example, are the losses speculative?

Specialist Legal Advice?

11.37 The supplier should consider obtaining specialist legal advice on the strength of their case.

Commercial Considerations

11.38 Does the supplier have their own cyber insurance which might cover them against any loss.

Set Litigation Strategy

11.39 The supplier will have to decide on the best strategy based on the legal, commercial and practical considerations in play.

Are they better settling early with the business so they can keep the legal costs at a minimum?

If the technology provider caused the breach, then they can be sued by the individuals affected by the data breach as well (processors can be sued for data security breaches under the GDPR – see **Chapter 1**).

Therefore, the technology provider may want to settle the action as quickly and quietly as possible and with a minimum of fuss or adverse publicity.

A Note on Privilege

11.40 Privilege is an important issue in commercial data protection litigation with technology providers. The most important evidence is usually emails and internal documents with employees in the company discussing the breach after it occurs. The question is whether these documents will see the light of day and be part of the discovery process. If the technology provider can assert legal privilege over the documents, then they may not have to disclose them to the claimant or the court.

Privilege is a complex area, but parties may be able to claim legal privilege over some of their documents.

Under English law there is litigation privilege and legal advice privilege.

Litigation privilege applies to confidential communications between a client and a professional legal adviser or a third party but only where litigation is contemplated or in progress.

Legal advice privilege applies to confidential communications between a client and a professional legal adviser for the purpose of obtaining legal advice.

In the aftermath of an incident both parties will wish to consider how they can best assert privilege over documents so they can protect their position in any subsequent litigation (or regulator action) relating to the technology provider data breach.

TAKEAWAYS

11.41

- **Due diligence** – Choose suppliers carefully and do due diligence on them before hiring them. Make sure they have the financial means to cover any losses.
- **Specialist legal advice** – Claimants and defendants in such actions against technology providers should obtain specialist legal advice as early as possible to help them navigate the case.
- **Contracts** – When hiring technology providers, companies should ensure the requirements around security are as precise as possible. Generic boiler plate clauses are no longer sufficient to deal with the evolving threat landscape.
- **Liabilities and indemnities** – When hiring a technology provider, a business should have clauses in place which covers it against all the losses that may rise in the event that the technology provider causes a data breach. These losses can be huge so it pays to ensure the wording in these clauses is watertight.

CHAPTER 12

Vicarious Liability and other Defences to Data Breach Claims

INTRODUCTION

12.01 In this chapter we consider:

- the concept of vicarious liability in data protection litigation, which usually arises where a rogue employee at a company causes a data breach. Vicarious liability considers the extent to which the company should be liable for the actions of their rogue employee; and
- the seminal case of *Various Claimants v VM Morrison Supermarkets*.[1]

We also consider some of the steps that claimants and defendants can take to protect their position if they are involved in data protection litigation involving potential vicarious liability issues.

PART 1
WHAT IS VICARIOUS LIABILITY?

12.02 Vicarious liability is 'a form of strict liability where an individual is responsible for the action or inaction of another person with whom they have a special relationship'.[2] An employer can be liable for the actions of its employee when they act in the scope of their employment.

PART 2
MORRISONS

12.03 In the case of *Various Claimants v VM Morrison Supermarkets*, a claim was brought by 9,263 Morrison employees for:

- breach of section 4(4) of the Data Protection Act 1998 (DPA 1998);
- misuse of private information; and
- breach of confidence.

1 *Various Claimants v VM Morrison Supermarkets* [2020] UKSC 12. For full judgment, see https://supremecourt.uk/uploads/WM_Morrison_Supermarkets_plc_*Appellant_v_Various_*Claimants_Respondents_e524b9da6f.pdf.

2 'Glossary', Practical Law, Thomson Reuters.

The data breach in this case pre-dated the GDPR hence the claimants sued under the DPA 1998.

The judicial intent behind this case is to show that employers are **not** automatically liable for rogue employees acting outside the scope of their employment.

In this case, a rogue employee seeking revenge on Morrisons uploaded personal data relating to Morrison's employees to the internet.

The Supreme Court overturned judgments of the High Court and the Court of Appeal and found that the supermarket giant was not liable for the actions of the rogue employee.

The table below sets out a summary of the vicarious liability concepts.

Case summary: ***Vicarious liability – Various Claimants v VM Morrison Supermarkets***	
Topic	*In Brief*
Introduction	• This 2020 Supreme Court case is the leading authority vicarious liability in data protection cases. • A rogue employee stole personal data relating to 9,263 employees from their employer and posted it on the internet.
Decision	• Morrisons was held to be not liable for the actions of its employee.
The test	• The test for establishing vicarious liability of employees is the 'closely connected' test. • Were the actions taken by the rogue employee so closely connected with his employment duties that they could be said to be done in the course of his employment?
Why was the rogue employee in Morrisons found to be acting on 'a frolic of his own'?	• The employee's actions arose out of a 'personal vendetta' he had against his employer. • They were nothing to do with his work duties.

THE CASE IN DETAIL

12.04 **Court:** Supreme Court

Date of judgment: 1 April 2020

Citation: [2020] UKSC 12

Factual Background

12.05

- The defendant in the original case was the UK supermarket giant Morrisons.
- The claimants were 9,263 of its employees or former employees.
- Personal information about them was published on the internet by another of Morrisons' employees, an individual we will call 'S'.
- In perhaps one of the stranger ironies in this case, S was a senior auditor in Morrisons' internal audit team.
- In July 2013, he was subject to disciplinary proceedings for minor misconduct and was given a verbal warning.[3]
- Thereafter, S had a grudge against Morrisons.
- To enable him to carry out some tasks relating to his internal audit work, he was given access to the payroll data relating to the whole of Morrisons' workforce – around 126,000 employees. These consisted of the name, address, gender, date of birth, phone numbers, national insurance number, bank sorting code, bank account number and salary of each member of staff.[4]
- He secretly copied this data onto a USB stick.
- As part of his vendetta against his employer, he uploaded the data of 100,000 Morrison employees onto the internet.
- He also sent CDs containing the files anonymously to three UK newspapers.
- He purported to be a concerned member of the public who had found the file on the file-sharing website.
- Within a few hours, Morrisons removed the data from the internet, informed its employees it had taken steps to ensure that the data was removed from the internet, instigated internal investigations, and informed the police.
- Soon afterwards, S was arrested and subsequently convicted of a number of offences and sentenced to eight years' imprisonment.
- Morrisons had spent more than £2.26 million in dealing with the immediate aftermath of the disclosure.[5]

RESULT

12.06 The Supreme Court found that Morrisons was not liable for the actions of its rogue employee.

3 *Various Claimants v VM Morrison Supermarkets*, paras 1–3.
4 *Ibid*, para 4.
5 *Ibid*, paras 1–8.

The Court found that: 'the circumstances in which S committed wrongs against the claimants were not such as to result in the imposition of vicarious liability upon his employer. Morrisons cannot therefore be held liable for S's conduct'.[6]

RATIONALE FOR DECISION

12.07 The Supreme Court found that the fact that the rogue employee's job gave him the opportunity to cause the breach isn't enough to establish vicarious liability.

The Court said: 'the mere fact that S's employment gave him the opportunity to commit the wrongful act would not be sufficient to warrant the imposition of vicarious liability'.[7]

IS THE EMPLOYEE'S BEHAVIOUR 'CLOSE ENOUGH' TO THEIR EMPLOYMENT DUTIES?

12.08 The Supreme Court set down a test for establishing whether the wrongful act was done in the course of his employment.

The Court said:

> the question is whether S's disclosure of the data was so closely connected with acts he was authorised to do that, for the purposes of the liability of his employer to third parties, his wrongful disclosure may fairly and properly be regarded as done by him while acting in the ordinary course of his employment.[8]

IS THE PERSON ACTING ON A FROLIC OF THEIR OWN/ INDEPENDENT PERSONAL VENTURE

12.09 Is the person acting 'on a frolic of their own' when they commit the wrongful act?

The Court said:

- The basic principle normally applicable to cases where an employee is engaged in an independent personal venture was explained in *Joel v Morison* (1834) 6 C & P 501, which concerned a claim for personal injuries brought by a plaintiff who had been knocked down by a cart driven by the defendant's employee.
- Judge Parke said at para 503 of *Joel v Morison* (1834):

  The master is only liable where the servant is acting in the course of his employment. If he was going out of his way, against his master's

6 *Ibid*, para 56.
7 *Ibid*, para 35.
8 *Ibid*, para 32.

> implied commands, when driving on his master's business, he will make his master liable; but if he was going on a frolic of his own, without being at all on his master's business, the master will not be liable.[9]

ON A PERSONAL VENDETTA?

12.10 In the *Morrisons* case, why was the employee held to be on a frolic of his own? The Court said this was because the employee was on a personal vendetta which had nothing to do with his work:

> In the present case, it is abundantly clear that S was not engaged in furthering his employer's business when he committed the wrongdoing in question. On the contrary, he was pursuing a personal vendetta, seeking vengeance for the disciplinary proceedings some months earlier ... S's wrongful conduct was not so closely connected with acts which he was authorised to do that, for the purposes of Morrisons' liability to third parties, it can fairly and properly be regarded as done by him while acting in the ordinary course of his employment.[10]

DOES DATA PROTECTION LEGISLATION EXCLUDE THE IMPOSITION OF VICARIOUS LIABILITY?

12.11 The Court rejected the defendant's submission that the DPA 1998 either expressly or impliedly excluded the vicarious liability of an employer.[11] Given the similarity of the security provisions in the DPA 1998 to those in the GDPR, this may leave the door open for potential vicarious liability claims in the future under the GDPR and the Data Protection Act 2018.

PART 3
PREVENTATIVE ACTION

Steps Companies can Take to Prevent Rogue Employees from Causing Data Breaches

12.12

- **Vetting** – Put in place appropriate vetting procedures and background checks on new employees before they are onboarded. Organisations that do this properly can save themselves a lot of pain and expense.
- **Policies** – Be clear in staff policies and employment contracts and staff training about what employees' duties are. Even if employees do 'go rogue' which leads to data protection litigation from other employees, then

9 *Ibid*, para 37.
10 *Ibid*, para 47.
11 *Ibid*, para 55.

employers can point to these things when trying to persuade the court that they are not responsible for the actions of the rogue employee.

- **Information security programme** – Companies must put technical controls in place to prevent rogue employees from exfiltrating personal data.

  Technical controls are vital in protecting against rogue employees. In the *Morrisons* case the rogue employee 'was given access to the payroll data relating to the whole of Morrisons' workforce: around 126,000 employees. These consisted of the name, address, gender, date of birth, phone numbers, national insurance number, bank sorting code, bank account number and salary of each member of staff'.[12] He 'surreptitiously copied the data from his work laptop on to a personal USB stick'.[13]

  With proper software and controls in place companies should be able to:

  - prevent data from being copies onto external media; and
  - monitor their network and prevent data from being sent outside it. Having proper cyber security controls in place is crucial.

TAKEAWAYS

Vicarious Liability Litigation – Tips

12.13

- **Establishing the facts** – If a rogue employee data case does occur, the parties must examine the evidence to see the extent to which any rogue employee was 'acting on a frolic of their own'.
- **Legal analysis** – The parties should obtain expert legal advice to establish the merits of any vicarious liability claim.
- **Gathering documents**
  - **Defendants** – Defendants should consider the extent to which their company documents suggest that the rogue employee was acting on a frolic of their own. For example, are there clear staff policies and contracts of employment which set out the employee duties. These may be useful in establishing that wrongful acts carried out by the rogue employee bore no relation to his employment duties.
  - **Claimants** – Claimants should try to ensure they have a strategy to obtain full discovery from the defendants as the paper trail may establish liability.
  - **Regulator decisions** – Has the Information Commissioner's Office (ICO) fined the employer for the breach? If so, then this will put the claimant in a stronger position.

12 *Ibid*, para 4.
13 *Ibid*, para 6.

CHAPTER 13

Cookie Litigation

INTRODUCTION

13.01 In this chapter we consider litigation that may arise when organisations breach the rules on cookies when processing the personal data of individuals. There are laws in place which prevent cookies from tracking the online browsing of individuals without their knowledge of consent.

As a result, people often feel 'banner fatigue' from having to click cookie notices when they use websites.

This chapter is split into four sections:

- What are cookies?
- What are the legal requirements on cookie use?
- Can claimants obtain compensation for breach of the cookie rules?
- Recent case law that may impact cookie litigation – cookies litigation is still nascent.

The legislative intent behind the cookies regulations are to prevent companies from using cookies to invade people's privacy by tracking, monitoring or surveilling them without their knowledge.

Executive summary table for this chapter	
Topic	*In brief*
What is a cookie?	A small text file downloaded onto a computer allowing website to store information about the user's preferences
How does the GDPR impact cookies?	If cookies process personal data, then it must be processed in line with the GDPR
Which other laws impact cookies?	The UK PECR rules say you must: • tell people the cookies are there • explain what the cookies are doing • get the person's consent
Cookies litigation examples	• Consent • Breach of the fair and lawful rules • Breach of the transparency rules • Profiling
Cookies litigation case law	• *Lloyd v Google LLC* [2021] UKSC 50 • *RTM v Bonne Terre Ltd & Anor* [2026] EWCA Civ 488

PART 1
INTRODUCTION TO COOKIES

What is a Cookie?

13.02 The Information Commissioner's Officer (ICO) says 'A cookie is a small file of letters and numbers that is downloaded on to your computer when you visit a website. Cookies are used by many websites and can do a number of things, eg remembering your preferences, recording what you have put in your shopping basket, and counting the number of people looking at a website.'[1]

A cookie is like the ID card that a user shows when they go back on a website. It tells the website owner that the user has returned.[2]

What is the Point of Cookies?

13.03 Cookies can:

- make the browsing experience more efficient;
- save customers time in having to login with each visit; and
- provide customers with information that is more relevant to them.

What Kinds of Cookies are there?

13.04 There are numerous kinds of cookies including:

- **Session cookies**[3] – These are cookies that are only stored on the user's browsing session. They are removed as soon as the browser is closed. The purpose of this cookie is to allow a person to move from one page to the next so without having to log in. For example, if a user puts something in their digital shopping basket whilst browsing on Amazon, then the cookie will allow the site to keep track of the items whilst the user is moving from page to page. These are the least privacy-invasive cookies.
- **Permanent cookies** – These are cookies which are stored permanently on the browser's site 'and are not deleted when the browser is closed …'. They are usually configured to keep track of users for a prolonged period, in some cases many years into the future'.[4] These cookies can therefore analyse user's browsing activity on the website over a prolonged or even permanent period. For example, Sean logs into a classic car website a few

1 ICO, 'Cookies and Similar Technologies', https://ico.org.uk/for-organisations/direct-marketing-and-privacy-and-electronic-communications/guide-to-pecr/cookies-and-similar-technologies/.
2 See the ICO recommended website – 'aboutcookies.org'.
3 aboutcookies.org.
4 'Permanent, persistent, or stored cookies', aboutcookies.org.

times and accesses the pages about classic Lamborghini cars. He closes his session and returns a year later. The website recognises the user and serves him up more details of Lamborghini cars.

Myths about Cookies

13.05

- **Cookies never collect personal data** – This myth is incorrect. Recital 30 of the GDPR says 'Natural persons may be associated with cookie identifiers'. When the information which cookies collect can be linked back to a person, then that person's personal data is processed by the cookies.
- **Cookies cannot track and profile people across multiple websites** – This myth is false. For example, Sean visits a classic car website, then a news site — and the same advertising cookie recognises him on both sites, linking his browsing behaviour together and building a profile about him.

PART 2
COOKIES AND DATA PROTECTION LAW

Do Cookies Process Personal Data?

13.06 Personal data is data which relates to an individual. This can include data like internet protocol (IP) addresses. An IP address is a unique number assigned to every device which uses the internet. Cookies often process data related to your device which can therefore be linked back to you.

Cookie Use Must be Consistent with GDPR Principles

13.07 GDPR may impact cookie use in numerous ways

When controllers use cookies, they must ensure that the data processing is consistent with the GDPR principles. When companies process personal data relating to cookies then they must do so in a manner which is consistent with the GDPR. For example, they must comply with the first GDPR principle on fairness and transparency. This means users need to be told about how cookies use their information in cookie notices.

Cookie use must be consistent with the GDPR rules on lawful bases

13.08 When companies process personal data, they need a lawful basis to process that personal data. For example, the company setting the cookies on the website may need one of the following lawful bases before they can set the cookies:

- consent;
- necessary for the performance of a contract; and
- legitimate interests.

The consent must be valid.

See **Chapter 1** for more details on the GDPR principles and the rules on lawful bases.

The PECR Rules

13.09 When companies use cookies, their cookie use must comply with the GDPR as well as another overlapping statutory regime called the Privacy and Electronic Communications (EC Directive) Regulations 2003 (PECR Regulations). PECR still applies post-Brexit. PECR is UK legislation which implements an EU Directive known as the 'E-Privacy Directive' which governs cookie usage.

The ICO says 'The rules on cookies are in regulation 6 (of PECR). The basic rules say that companies must:

- Tell people the cookies are there
- Explain what the cookies are doing and why, and
- Get the person's consent to store a cookie on their device.'[5]

Cookies must not be installed until the company has obtained the appropriate consent from the website user.

They must provide enough information on the site near the cookie consent to explain how the cookie data is processed.

The consent required is the GDPR standard of consent under Article 7.

The consent must be:

- freely given;
- specific;
- informed; and
- opt in.

5 ICO, Cookies and similar technologies, https://ico.org.uk/for-organisations/direct-marketing-and-privacy-and-electronic-communications/guide-to-pecr/cookies-and-similar-technologies/.

In the EU case of *Planet49*,[6] the Court of Justice of the European Union (CJEU) found that:

- Pre-ticked boxes allowing the use of cookies is not consent.
- The requirement for consent stands whether the cookie is processing personal data or not.
- Cookie notices should tell people whether third parties can access the cookie information.

CJEU decisions which were decided pre-Brexit (like the *Planet49* case which was decided in 2019 before Brexit took effect in 2020) still guide UK courts when interpreting UK law.

Companies can be fined up to £17.5 million or 4% of their annual turnover for breaches of the cookie rules under new legislation in the Data Use and Access Act 2025.

In *RTM v Bonne Terre Ltd & ICO*, a case in the Court of Appeal which we consider in more detail below, Lord Justice Warby summed up the law within PECR. He said:[7]

> - PECR was enacted some five years after the DPA 1998.
> - Regulations 6 and 22 prohibit the use of cookies or the sending of direct marketing emails without consent.
> - Regulation 30 of PECR provides that a person who suffers damage by reason of a contravention of PECR shall be entitled to bring proceedings for compensation.

Similar Technologies are also Covered by the Cookie Rules

13.10 The ICO goes on to say:

> regulation 6 applies to anyone who stores information on a user's device or gains access to information on a user's device, in either case by any method.
>
> This means the same rules apply to any similar technologies – such as Local Shared Objects (sometimes called Flash cookies) – and can also cover other types of technology, including apps on smartphones.[8]

6 Case C-673/17, *Planet49*, ECLI:EU:C:2019:801.
7 *RTM v Bonne Terre Ltd & ICO*, paras 18–21.
8 ICO, 'Cookies and Similar Technologies', https://ico.org.uk/for-organisations/direct-marketing-and-privacy-and-electronic-communications/guide-to-pecr/cookies-and-similar-technologies/.

PART 3
HOW DO THE COOKIES RULES LEAD TO COOKIES LITIGATION

13.11 If the law on cookies (either in the UK GDPR or PECR) are infringed, then individuals may be able to sue for compensation.

For example, potential court actions that individuals have taken related to cookies include:

- breach of the rules on consent – eg, that the cookie was placed withier without consent or with an invalid consent (see *RTM v Bonne Terre*);
- breach of the fair and lawful rules – eg, cookies tracked the user in ways which were unfair to them;
- breach of the transparency rules – eg, the cookies processed personal data behind the claimant's back; and
- profiling – eg, cookies were used to build profiles of individuals.

Claiming Damage in Cookies Cases

13.12 As we discussed in **Chapter 2** on damages, when claimants sue for compensation in a data protection case, they must be able to show:

- breach of data protection law – eg, breach of GDPR or PECR in terms of the way cookies operated;
- material or non-material damage – eg, damage or distress caused to the claimant due to cookie use; and
- causation – eg, the damage was linked to the cookie use.

The main challenge in cookies cases might be showing damage (eg, was the collection or processing of the data via cookies such that it caused damage or distress).

PART 4
COOKIES CASES

RTM v Bonne Terre Ltd & ICO [2026] EWCA Civ 488[9]

13.13 **Court**: Court of Appeal

Date: 21 April 2026

9 https://www.judiciary.uk/wp-content/uploads/2026/04/RTM-v-Bonne-Terre-2026-EWCA-Civ-488.pd

- SBG operates an online betting and gaming business under the trading name 'Sky Betting and Gaming'.
- RTM was a problem gambler and his identity was anonymised in the proceedings.
- By early 2019 he had overcome his problem.
- SBG placed cookies on RTM's devices or his browser, processed his personal data, and sent him targeted direct marketing
- RTM used SBG's services and lost sums of money.
- RTM later sued SBG for compensation and declarations, contending that he was a gambling addict and that SBG had acted unlawfully in its:
  - placement of cookies,
  - it's processing of his personal data; and
  - its direct marketing communications.
- He said this caused him to gamble more and to lose more than he would otherwise have done, and that he had thereby suffered financial loss and distress.
- He brought a claim in privacy and data protection.[10]

The use of cookies – objective test on consent

13.14

- The defendant used sophisticated technology and data processing including 'building propensity models – using individuals … past behaviour to predict their future behaviour'.[11]
- Mrs Justice Collins Rice in the High Court said 'The Claimant's consenting behaviours proceeded directly from a damaged and defective condition of personal autonomy' such that his consent was not valid.[12]
- The defendant's 'use of cookies … were not lawful processing … The profiling was parasitic on the obtaining of the data and the ultimate delivery of the marketing, and had no other standalone purpose so far as he was concerned'.[13]
- This was overturned in the Court of Appeal. Lord Justice Warby said:
  - 'I disagree with the judge's legal analysis … I therefore conclude that the judge's decision on liability is vitiated by error of law.[14]

10 *RTM v Bonne Terre Ltd & ICO* [2026] EWCA Civ 488, para 4.
11 *RTM v Bonne Terre* [2025] EWHC 111 (KB), para 81.
12 *Ibid*, para 204.
13 *Ibid*, para 205.
14 *RTM v Bonne Terre Ltd & ICO* [2026] EWCA Civ 488, para 10.

   - The question … is whether the data subject has "given" consent to the processing or other activity.[15]
   - These are purely objective questions about the quality and significance of some identifiable communication by the data subject to the data controller. Typically, this will be by ticking a box or some similar act.[16]
   - The data controller must also prove to the necessary standard that the data subject's "indication" met each of the four criteria prescribed by the legislation, namely that it was (i) freely given, (ii) specific, (iii) informed, and (iv) unambiguous.
   - Each of these criteria is also objective in nature.[17]
   - A decision on whether the four criteria were probably satisfied will require an assessment of the data subject's "indication" in its context including, in particular, the communications between the data subject and the data controller, and the structural character of the relationship between them.
   - To prove consent, the data controller does not have to prove what was actually in the mind of the individual data subject at the time of the "indication".[18]
   - It is neither necessary nor relevant for this purpose to explore whether the individual data subject was vulnerable, with an impaired ability to make fully autonomous decisions.[19]
   - The application of the concept of consent may depend on the context. For instance, a statement that would be "unambiguous" when made to an adult audience might not have that quality when made to children. But the concept of consent must be uniform for all purposes, regardless of the particular factual matrix of the individual case, or the business or other context in which the question is raised.[20]
   - The case must be remitted to the High Court.[21]
   - RTM still has claims that SBG's processing of his data was unfair, and infringed other data protection principles, that remain to be resolved'.[22]
- Result: Claimant was unsuccessful in showing that his consent for cookies on the defendant's website was invalid.

15 *Ibid*, para 9.
16 *Ibid*, para 9.
17 *Ibid*, para 9.
18 *Ibid*, para 10.
19 *Ibid*, para 9.
20 *Ibid*, para 53.
21 *Ibid*, para 96.
22 *Ibid*, para 98.

Lloyd v Google LLC [2021] UKSC 50

13.15 **Court**: Supreme Court[23]

Date: 10 November 2021

Type of group litigation: Representative action[24]

Number of claimants: Estimated at 4 million.[25]

Cause of action: Breach of section 4(4) of the Data Protection Act 1998 (DPA 1998)[26]

Result: Claim unsuccessful. Breach of the DPA 1998 needed proof of actual damage not mere loss of control of information.[27]

Factual background

13.16 Whilst this case didn't concern cookies directly, it concerned cookie-style tracking.

The claimants alleged that, for several months in late 2011 and early 2012, Google secretly tracked the internet activity of millions of Apple iPhone users and used the data collected in this way for commercial purposes without the users' knowledge or consent. This was possible through the alleged use of the 'Safari workaround' to bypass privacy settings on Apple iPhones.[28]

The basis for the claimants' action was breach of the fair and lawfulness principle of DPA 1998.[29]

The claimants argued that there was a base level of harm that affected all claimants. The court's view was that this didn't work when the base level of harm didn't reach the threshold required for damages.[30]

23 https://caselaw.nationalarchives.gov.uk/ewhc/kb/2025/490.
24 *Lloyd v Google LLC*, para 5.
25 *Ibid*, para 5.
26 *Ibid*, para 1.
27 *Ibid*, para 159.
28 *Ibid*, para 9.
29 *Ibid*, paras 1 and 18.
30 *Ibid*, paras 145–147.

TAKEAWAYS

13.17

- **Cookie claims** – Cookies litigation is possible on a number of fronts including when the use of cookies breaches the GDPR rules on:
  - consent – eg, the cookie was placed without valid consent;
  - breach of the fair and lawful rules – eg, the cookies tracked the user in ways which were unfair;
  - breach of the transparency rules – eg, the cookie processed data without telling people about this; and
  - profiling – eg, cookies were used to build profiles of individuals.
- **Proof of damage needed** – The claimant must prove that the cookies rules were breached and that this caused the claimant some form of damage to them such as distress.
- **Group claims on cookies still possible** – Successful group litigation on tracking technology has had its wings clipped in *Lloyd v Google*. However, it is still possible for cookies litigation to succeed.

CHAPTER 14

How the Use of AI can Trigger Data Protection Litigation

INTRODUCTION

14.01 The chapter covers:

- the main principles around artificial intelligence (AI);
- basic understanding of AI concepts;
- how data protection rights and freedoms may be impacted by AI;
- reducing the risks of AI;
- two data protection cases in the UK with an AI-technology background; and
- how UK AI-related litigation may develop in the future and future proofing.

AI is a vast subject. This chapter can only introduce some of the main concepts around AI. The chapter focusses on the impact of AI on UK data protection litigation.

AI chapter summary table	
Topic	*In brief*
AI jargon buster	• **Gen AI** – AI which creates new content such as new images and video • **Machine learning** – the component in AI technology which allows the AI to learn and improve its outputs • **Training data** – data sets used to teach AI models how to find pattern and make predictions • **Hallucinations** – AI makes up false or inaccurate information • **AI bias** – AI outputs which have discriminatory effects on people • **Large language model** – network of algorithms which can understand and respond to human language • **Explainability** – ability to make AI decision-making process understandable to humans • **Human in the loop** – AI outputs decisions which are not fully automated but are overseen by humans • **Black box effect –** AI decision-making process is unknown • **Anonymisation** – turning personal data into anonymous information

Topic	*In brief*
Types of data protection claims in AI – examples	AI may breach the GDPR in numerous ways including: • fair and lawful rule, eg, AI system makes decision which is unfair • transparency rule, eg, people have no notice that AI is processing their personal data • accuracy rule, eg AI produces outputs based on inaccurate personal data • automated decision making, eg, there is no human oversight of AI decision which breaches Article 22 of the GDPR • security rule, eg, personal data in AI system are hacked • right of access, eg, claimant makes data subject access request and defendant cannot access the personal data in the AI system
Case law	Cases where the use of AI triggered data protection litigation: • *Prismall v Google UK Ltd* [2024] EWCA Civ 1516 • *RTM v Bonne Terre Ltd & Anor* [2026] EWCA Civ 488

WHAT IS AI?

14.02 AI is an umbrella term which covers different types of technology that can imitate human learning, reasoning, and logic.

The Oxford Dictionary defines artificial intelligence (AI) as: 'the theory and development of computer systems able to perform tasks normally requiring human intelligence, such as:

- visual perception
- speech recognition
- decision-making, and
- translation between languages.'

AI can comprise both computer hardware (the physical machines) and software (the computer programs on those machines).

However, as the definition of AI has developed over time, AI is increasingly thought of as software rather than hardware.

WHAT IS THE DIFFERENCE BETWEEN AN AI MODEL AND AN AI SYSTEM

14.03 An AI model is the algorithm which has been trained to provide outputs. This is like the engine in a plane.

An AI system is the finished AI product which may be made up of multiple AI models as well as data and other software.

An AI system is like the finished plane which is ready to fly.

AI BENEFITS

14.04 AI benefits include:

- forecasting (eg, a retail company anticipating what the sales will be in the run up to Christmas);
- recommendation (eg, Amazon recommending books that a customer might like based on past purchases); and
- optimization (eg, an Uber app figuring out the best route to avoid traffic).

PART I
UNDERSTANDING THE BASICS ON AI

14.05 If claimant lawyers have a good understanding of AI technology, they can leverage that knowledge to interrogate the defendants about how the personal data was used in the AI system, hopefully, to the benefit of their clients.

There are many different types of AI.

For example, the European Parliament[1] says there are two main categories – software AI and embedded AI.

Software AI includes:

- virtual assistants (such as the software that powers your Alexa device or your predictive text messaging on WhatsApp); and
- internet search engines (such as Google search).

Embodied AI is where the AI is inside a physical object. Examples include:

- robots (eg, the AI Robot 'Sparrow' which is a robotic arm which Amazon uses to identify, handle, sort, and store products);[2]
- self-driving cars (eg, the Tesla autopilot feature);
- drones (eg, such as those used by the US military); and
- Internet of Things (IoT) (eg, a smart home device which adjusts your heating automatically in response to the weather forecast).

1 European Parliament, 'What is AI and how is it used?'.
2 'Amazon introduces Sparrow', Aboutamazon.com, 10 November 2022.

PART 2
AI JARGON BUSTER

14.06 In this section we examine some of the key concepts in AI which may arise in data protection litigation. This is only a brief overview. AI technology is a vast and developing area and we can only scratch the surface of the technology in this chapter.

What is Generative AI?

14.07 Generative AI creates new content such as new images and text.

What is the difference between Generative AI (or 'Gen AI') and traditional AI? Traditional AI might be able to recognise an apple and categorise it. Generative AI can create or generate an image of an apple.

ChatGPT is an example of Generative AI.

What is Machine Learning

14.08 Machine Learning or 'ML' is an important component in AI technology. It is the technology which allows the AI to learn and improve its outputs and decisions.

It is a subset of AI that enables computers to learn and improve independently. It 'focusses on developing computer programs that can learn trends and patterns from data to make predictions or optimizations'.[3]

Machine learning works by identifying trends and patterns in data sets. Over time the machine learning algorithm collects more data, and it continuously learns from the new data and the patterns it has previously identified. As a result, the machine learning can make better and more accurate predictions, and it can do so independently of human beings.

- In supervised machine learning, the system is supervised by the human beings developing the system. The humans babysit and oversee the program.
- The AI system will be given more examples in terms of the patterns it should find.
- With unsupervised machine learning, the system acts with more autonomy and there is less input from humans.
- The algorithm is free to look at the data independently at the data and to find patterns within the data on its own.

3 'Glossary Term, Machine Learning', Practical Law, Thomson Reuters, http://uk.practicallaw.thomsonreuters.com.

What is Natural Language Processing?

14.09 Natural language processing or 'NLP' is another subset of AI that allows computers to understand and respond to human language. ChatGPT uses NLP and is therefore able to understand your queries and respond to them.

Training Data

14.10 These are the vast numbers of data sets used to teach AI models how to find pattern and make predictions.

The training is a large reservoir of different types of data that may include structured and unstructured data including text and images. Much of that data may be personal data although AI can also process other non-personal information, such as factual data (such as weather information) or confidential information such as data relating to a company's financial performance.

For example, if you want visual perception AI to recognise images of roses, then it is estimated that you need to train the model with up to 25,000 images of roses before it is able to recognise the image properly. High volumes of training data are essential to AI. However, the vast quantities of data can bring the AI into conflict with law and regulation when the AI is processing of personal data.

The model is trained on this data before it is 'deployed' (ie, released into the public domain).

Large Language Models (LLMs)

14.11 LLMs are large networks of algorithms which can understand human language and respond to it in human language. They use machine learning to allow them to learn from input data to generate better responses.

Hallucinations

14.12 An AI hallucination occurs when the AI (usually LLMs) makes up false or inaccurate information when providing outputs. The danger with hallucinations is that they can often seem very plausible.

AI Bias

14.13 AI systems may produce biased or unfair outputs. The Information Commissioner's Office (ICO) has said 'AI systems learn from data which may be unbalanced and/or reflect discrimination, they may produce outputs which have discriminatory effects on people based on their gender, race, age, health, religion, disability, sexual orientation or other characteristics.'[4]

For example, in December 2023, the pharmacy chain Rite Aid in the US was banned from using AI facial recognition software for a period of five years.[5] AI facial recognition software had wrongly and disproportionately identified ethnic minorities and women as shoplifters. Some customers were followed round the store, asked to leave and the police were called. The software produced biased outputs that discriminated against these groups.

AI Outputs

14.14 This is the result or response given by an AI system after entering in the input data (eg, the answer that ChatGPT provides when a user asks a question).

Explainability

14.15 The refers to the ability to make AI decision-making process understandable to humans, thus:

- companies must be able to explain their AI processing to customers, clients, employees and regulators; and
- people have legal rights to receive explanations of AI processing if the AI system processes personal data (see below).

The Black Box Effect

14.16 Sometimes we do not know how AI makes decisions. For example, if AI turns someone down for a job or identifies them as a suspect in a police investigation, then it is important for those people to understand how and why the AI came to its decision. Sometimes the AI decision-making process is so complex that it is hidden or unknown even to the AI system developer. In other words, no one knows what is happening in the black box. This can infringe people's GDPR rights on fairness and transparency.

4 ICO, 'What about fairness, bias and discrimination?', https://ico.org.uk/for-organisations/uk-gdpr-guidance-and-resources/artificial-intelligence/guidance-on-ai-and-data-protection/how-do-we-ensure-fairness-in-ai/what-about-fairness-bias-and-discrimination/.

5 'Rite Aid's A.I. Facial Recognition Wrongly Tagged People of Color as Shoplifters', *New York Times*, 21 December 2023.

Human in the Loop

14.17 This is a system where AI outputs decisions that are not fully automated but are overseen, and if necessary, overruled by humans. Having a documented Human in the loop (HITL) process reduces legal risk.

Anonymisation

14.18 This is the process of turning personal data into anonymous information, so that no one can be identified by it. Anonymisation can be used to reduce risk in AI models.

PART 3
HOW DO AI SYSTEMS PROCESS DATA?

14.19 AI systems process data in the following stages:

(1) **Collection** – data are gathered from many sources including web scraping from the internet.

(2) **Training** – large data sets are used to build the AI model. Training is what happens before the model is deployed. The training data then becomes an integral part of the AI model.

(3) **Learning** – the model is updated and refined by collecting new data after deployment to improve the AI models outputs. For example, when you tell Netflix that you like a movie whilst watching, that allows Netflix to update the film recommendation it sends to you. Training is not to be confused with learning in AI. Training is pre-deployment; learning occurs after deployment when the AI system has been released into the world.

(4) **Outputs** – the AI provides results such as text or a generated image. For example, when you ask ChatGPT a question and it gives you a text answer that is the output.

(5) **Feedback** – the AI system records feedback from the system users. This helps it correct mistakes and further refine the model. For example, if chatbot users flag answers that are wrong or unhelpful, that is feedback.

DATA PROTECTION

14.20 As we have seen, data protection law regulates the processing of personal data. The GDPR is the kingpin of the EU and UK data protection regime.[6] Data protection law regulates the processing of personal data. AI often involves the processing of large quantities of personal data.

6 Regulation (EU) 2016/679 (General Data Protection Regulation).

Personal data under the GDPR are data that relate to an identified or an identifiable human being.

PART 4
HOW COULD DATA PROCESSING IN AI LEAD TO DATA PROTECTION CLAIMS

Myth Busting

Myth 1 – It is impossible for a claimant to prove liability against a defendant in a data protection claim involving AI because the technology is so complex

14.21 This is incorrect. The developers of AI systems cannot hide behind the complexity of the AI system to escape liability in claims for breach of data protection law.

Claimants have several legal rights at their disposal which put the onus on companies that use AI to provide answers to individuals about how their data is processed in AI models. These rights include:

- the right of access (under Article 15 of GDPR);
- the right to be informed about how their personal data are used (Article 13 of GDPR); and
- the right to ask for information about the logic a computer used when making a decision (under Articles 15 and 22 of the GDPR).

These rights allow individuals to ask companies to provide them with copies of their data and information about how it was used on an AI model. If the companies cannot provide individuals with answers about this, then those individuals can sue the companies for breach of their GDPR rights.

Myth 2 – AI class actions for breach of data protection will be huge in the UK

14.22 This remains to be seen. Group claims are still difficult to get off the ground in the UK (see **Chapter 10**) due to the rules relating to group litigation orders and representative actions.

However, AI can breach data protection in numerous different ways.

The main grounds for AI claims are likely to be:

- breach of fairness rules (eg, the AI system discriminates against a particular ethnic group);
- breach of security (eg, the AI system being hacked); or

- breach of transparency (ie, the company using AI to process personal data behind people's backs).

Even if an AI system causes mass harm, such as an AI CV-scanning tool which discriminates against large numbers of people, claimant lawyers will still have the same hurdles to overcome as in other group litigation.

EIGHT MAIN WAYS IN WHICH DATA PROCESSING IN AI CAN LEAD TO LITIGATION

14.23 There are probably eight main ways in which the GDPR rules can be infringed using AI, namely, by breach of the GDPR rules on:

(1) lawful processing;

(2) transparency;

(3) accuracy;

(4) bias;

(5) computer decision-making;

(6) security;

(7) GDPR rights; and

(8) data minimisation.

Below we consider how AI technology can potentially breach these GDPR rules and therefore lead to litigation.

Unlawful Processing

Fair and lawful – Article 5(1)(a)

14.24

This is a very wide rule in the GDPR.

Companies processing personal data must process data in AI models fairly and lawfully. They must:

- identify a valid legal basis for processing personal data;
- process data in a way which is compliant with other laws; and
- process data in a way that individuals would reasonably expect.

How AI impacts this rule

14.25 This is one of the real challenges of AI processing. Any company that is processing personal data needs a legal basis under the GDPR to do so. Often companies process the personal data of people with whom they have no relationship. AI systems are often trained on personal data they obtain from web scraping. This can include personal data. If the company doing the web scraping is collecting it from strangers, then they may not have a legal basis to process that data or to use it within an AI model.

Before an organisation can process a person's personal data, they need a solid and justifiable legal basis under Article 6 of the GDPR to process the personal data of an individual. The ICO says *'whenever you are processing personal data – whether to train a new AI system, or make predictions using an existing one – you must have an appropriate lawful basis to do so.'* Potential legal bases include consent, contractual necessity, and legitimate interest of your firm. If you are processing special category data within the AI system (such as data relating to health or ethnicity), then companies need a further legal basis under Article 9 of the GDPR, such as gaining the 'explicit consent' of these individuals).

Example of how that may play out in litigation

14.26 Unlawful processing is likely to be one of the most prominent grounds for AI litigation.

Lack of Transparency

GDPR rule – Article 5(1)(a)

14.27 Personal data must be processed transparently.

How AI impacts this rule

14.28 As AI algorithms become more complex, it can be harder to explain them to individuals.

Example of how that may play out in litigation

14.29 For example:

- A bank uses AI software to decide on loan applications.
- When customers apply for a bank loan, their data goes into the AI software which then decides whether to refuse the loan.

- Many customers have asked how their personal data is processed in the tool.
- The bank is unable to provide answers as it does not fully understand the logic of the AI.
- As a result, some claimant solicitors wish to take a collective action on behalf of hundreds of claimants because the bank was not sufficiently transparent about how their data was processed.
- The claimant solicitors argue that the bank's use of AI has breached GDPR.

Inaccurate AI Decisions

GDPR rule – Article 5(1)(d)

14.30 Personal data must be kept accurate and up to date.

How AI impacts this rule

14.31 AI can rely on inaccurate data, leading to incorrect decisions about people. This can infringe the GDPR rule on accuracy.

Example of how that may play out in litigation

14.32 This is likely to be key in AI litigation.

For example:

- Dave Applies for a promotion with Real Corp a large UK IT company.
- The AI model processes obsolete data relating to Dave's old CV.
- As a result of this, Dave is turned down for promotion.
- Dave sues Real Corp alleging that AI processed inaccurate data causing him loss and damage.

Biased Decisions

GDPR rule – Article 5(1)(d)

14.33 Personal data must be kept accurate.

How AI impacts this rule

14.34 This rule means that AI decisions using personal data must be free from bias.

Example of how that may play out in litigation

14.35

- The *New York Times* reported a case in the US where in December 2023, the pharmacy chain Rite Aid was banned from using AI facial recognition software for a period of five years.[7]
- Rite Aid used AI facial recognition software which had wrongly and disproportionately identified particular ethnic groups as shoplifters.
- Some customers were followed round the store, asked to leave and the police were called.
- The AI software produced biased outputs that discriminated against these groups.

When AI technology is used, entities must ensure that they process data in a fair, lawful and transparent way.

If such a case happened in the UK, then the person may be able to sue under the rule that personal data must be accurate and free from bias.

Automated Decision-making

GDPR rule – Article 22

14.36 Article 22 of the GDPR says: 'The data subject shall have the right not to be subject to a decision based solely on automated processing, including profiling, which produces legal effects concerning him or her or similarly significantly affects him or her.'

These are known as the automated decision-making or 'ADM' rules.

How AI impacts this rule

14.37 The ICO says:

> The UK GDPR has provisions on: automated individual decision-making (making a decision solely by automated means without any human involvement) …
>
> You must identify whether any of your processing falls under Article 22 and, if so, make sure that you:
>
> - give individuals information about the processing
> - introduce simple ways for them to request human intervention or challenge a decision

7 'Rite Aid's A.I. Facial Recognition Wrongly Tagged People of Color as Shoplifters', *New York Times*, 21 December 2023.

- carry out regular checks to make sure that your systems are working as intended.

For example, if an AI system does produce an output which has a significant effect on a person (such as refusing them for a job or a bank loan), then that person may be able to sue for breach of their rights under Article 22 of GDPR.

Example of how that may play out in litigation

14.38 We saw this arise in a case in the Netherlands case instigated by taxi drivers against Uber. The defendant was alleged to have fired the taxi drivers from their jobs and using an AI system to make the decision on which drivers should be fired. Some of the taxi drivers took claims against Uber for breach of the GDPR.

In 2023, the Court of Appeal in the Netherlands upheld the claims of the taxi drivers.

Whilst Uber claimed that humans reviewed the decisions, the Court found that the human reviews were superficial.

The drivers' rights under the ADM rules in the GDPR, article 22 had been infringed.[8]

Security Breaches

GDPR rule – Article 5(1)(f)

14.39 Companies must ensure personal data must be kept securely with appropriate organisational and technical measures in place.

How AI impacts this rule

14.40 Is AI technology more prone to being hacked than other technologies? Whilst we may not be able to answer this question definitively, AI can often lead to data breaches. As the ICO says 'Some of the unique characteristics of AI mean compliance with data protection law's security requirements can be more challenging than with other, more established technologies, both from a technological and human perspective.'[9]

8 https://fountaincourt.uk/2023/04/amsterdam-court-upholds-appeal-in-algorithmic-decision-making-test-case-drivers-v-uber-and-ola/.

9 https://ico.org.uk/for-organisations/uk-gdpr-guidance-and-resources/artificial-intelligence/guidance-on-ai-and-data-protection/how-should-we-assess-security-and-data-minimisation-in-ai/.

The huge pools of personal data within an AI model can be an attractive honeypot for hackers. We have seen examples of large tech companies training data sets being a target for hackers.

AI can also have security vulnerabilities which means that the data within AI models can be hacked. For example, some hackers use a process called model inversion to get at the personal data within the AI model. This is where hackers use a model outputs to infer sensitive information from its training data. It involves querying the model and looking at the outputs to try and infer the personal data in the model.

In one reported case, there were reports that a tech giant AI tool was exploited by hackers who put malicious prompts into it and was able to expose the data of nearly one million users.[10]

Example of how that may play out in litigation

14.41 An AI software database is hacked. The details of thousands of individuals go out into the wild. Claimant solicitors start a group action to get compensation for the individuals affected.

Data Rights

14.42 Under data protection law, individuals have numerous rights over their personal data including:

- the right to be informed;
- the right of access – including a right to access information about how the AI model made its decision; [11]
- the right to rectification;
- the right to erasure;
- the right to restrict processing;
- the right to data portability;
- the right to object; and
- the rights related to automated decision-making including profiling.

(See GDPR, Articles 12–22 for details on rights.)

Individuals can make requests to companies relating to these rights such as a request to:

10 'Hacker Exposes Amazon Q Security Flaws Using Covert Code', 28 July 2025, https://www.techrepublic.com/article/news-amazon-q-data-wiping-prompt-security-hack/.
11 GDPR, Article 15(1)(h).

- access a copy of their data (a right to access request); or
- erase their data (a right to erasure request).

How AI impacts these rules

14.43 It is very challenging for companies using AI to comply with these rights. These rights give individuals extensive rights and control over their personal data within AI models.

How this might play out in litigation

14.44 For example, let's imagine that a global company uses an AI model to build profiles of millions of their employees which it then uses to help it review employee performance.

The AI model is trained on data relating to those employees. Eva is one of those employees and works in the UK. She makes a GDPR subject access request for a copy of her data. She also asks to access details about how the AI model came to its decision about her performance. The company is unable to find Eva's data because the model is so big and complex. Eva sues for breach of her GDPR rights.

Breach of the GDPR Data Minimisation Principle

GDPR rule –Article 5(1)(c)

14.45 The data minimisation principle requires companies to process the minimum amount of personal data needed to fulfil their goal, and to only process that information, and no more.

How AI impacts this rule

14.46 AI systems process vast amounts of data. However, if AI systems process excessive data, this may offend the data minimisation rule.

Example of how that may play out in litigation

14.47 For example:

- Rafiq asks a social media company for access to the data it processed on him.
- The company produces copies of vast quantities of data it processed on him in various AI models.

- Rafiq believes this breaches the GDPR data minimisation principle and he sues the social media company for compensation.

PART 5
REGULATOR DECISIONS

ICO and Clearview AI[12]

14.48

- In May 2022, the ICO fined Clearview AI £7.5 million for using images of people in the UK in AI facial recognition software that were collected from the web and social media to create a global online database.
- Clearview AI collected more than 20 billion people images from the internet.
- The company provides an AI facial recognition technology which allowed its clients to upload a facial image of a person and then to check it for a match against images in a database.
- Clearview AI appealed the fine and enforcement notice to decision top the first-tier tribunal.
- The ICO then appealed that decision to the Upper Tribunal which upheld three of the ICO's four grounds of appeal.
- The ICO said 'The Upper Tribunal's decision has upheld our ability to protect UK residents from having their data, including images, unlawfully scraped and then used in a global online database without their knowledge.'
- The extent of the fine imposed by the ICO shows that unlawful processing (ie, processing personal data without having a lawful basis in place in AI technology) is a key priority for the ICO.

PART 6
LOOKING FORWARD – HOW MIGHT DATA PROTECTION LITIGATION IN THE UK RELATING TO AI DEVELOP?

14.49 The US litigation market is often a forerunner for how some aspects of litigation may develop in the UK. However, AI litigation in the UK is still in its infancy.

We are seeing some trends arise in the US including:

12 https://webarchive.nationalarchives.gov.uk/ukgwa/20220527163141/https://ico.org.uk/about-the-ico/news-and-events/news-and-blogs/2022/05/ico-fines-facial-recognition-database-company-clearview-ai-inc/.

- **Chatbot litigation** – There is a wave of chatbot litigation in the US. Many lawsuits have been filed relating to privacy issues with AI chatbots recording chats and monitoring people's behaviour in a way that infringes privacy laws. There was one allegation where the chat bot did not adequately respond when a teen expressed views relating to self-harm.[13]
- **Bias litigation** – We are seeing a rise in cases in the US where individuals are suing companies for making unfair decisions about them using AI. For example, a man claimed that a well-known AI screening tool was biased against him. The individual submitted over 100 job applications and he was rejected every time. He states it was on grounds of his race and age. A US federal court has allowed the case to go forward as a collective action.[14]
- **Biometric litigation** – These cases concern AI tools using facial recognition and voice analysis without the knowledge or consent of the individuals.

FUTURE PROOFING ON AI

14.50 Companies can put robust controls in place to protect against data protection litigation relating to AI. These may include:

- **Audit**

  Companies should audit their AI systems. All AI risk is not created equal. Identify higher risk AI tools which could cause the most damage if they malfunction.
- **Staff training**

  Staff should receive training on the proper use of AI.
- **Updating privacy notices to tell people about AI processing**
- **Conducting privacy risk assessment on AI before it is deployed**

  A data protection impact assessment (DPIA) is a risk assessment to assess any personal data processing and to ensure that appropriate mitigations are in place. The ICO has said 'in most cases, you are legally required to complete a DPIA if you use AI systems that process personal data. DPIAs offer you an opportunity to consider how and why you are using AI systems to process personal data and what the potential risks should be'.

  Companies must ensure they perform DPIAs on AI systems if personal data are used within the AI system. This should be carried out right at the start of the project to ensure data protection design and default are baked into the AI system right from the beginning.

13 'Character.AI and Google agree to settle lawsuits over teen mental health harms and suicides', 13 January 2026, https://edition.cnn.com/2026/01/07/business/character-ai-google-settle-teen-suicide-lawsuit.

14 Holland and Knight, 'Federal Court Allows Collective Action Lawsuit Over Alleged AI Hiring Bias', 27 May 2025.

- **Anonymising the personal data used in the AI model**

  Anonymised data is data which has been 'rendered anonymous in such a manner that the data subject is not or is no longer identifiable'. Anonymised data are outside the scope of the GDPR. If you can achieve the same aims on the AI project with anonymised data, then you should anonymise the data.

- **Policies, procedures, and training**

  Put staff policies in place which set out how your company will use AI responsibly.

- **Technical controls**

  Putting technical controls in place to prevent staff from doing foolish things with AI.

  For example:

  - blocking the use of unapproved AI that has not been approved so that staff cannot access these sites; and
  - using software to prevent your staff from uploading personal information into AI models.

TAKEAWAYS

14.51

- **Data and AI litigation** – The interface between AI technology and data protection litigation is complex. This is still a developing area. The way in which US litigation has developed may give some clues on how it may develop in the UK.
- **Multiple ways** – There are multiple ways in which a claimant could establish a claim under the GDPR in relation to the way in which data was processed in an AI model, including:
  - processing in an AI model without a valid legal basis;
  - subjecting a claimant to a decision made by AI which was unfair or biased; or
  - compromising the security of a claimant's data because the AI model used was hacked.

Index

[*all references are to paragraph number*]